DISCERN THE TIME

Can You Hear the Call to be Positioned for Purpose?

Sarah Holloway

Pr●Visi●n

Scripture quotations marked (NIV) are taken from the Holy Bible, New International Version®, NIV®. Copyright © 1973, 1978, 1984, 2011 by Biblica, Inc.® Used by permission of Zondervan. All rights reserved worldwide. www.zondervan.com The "NIV" and "New International Version" are trademarks registered in the United States Patent and Trademark Office by Biblica, Inc.®
"Scripture quotations are from The ESV® Bible (The Holy Bible, English Standard Version®), copyright © 2001 by Crossway, a publishing ministry of Good News Publishers. Used by permission. All rights reserved."
Scripture taken from the New King James Version®. Copyright © 1982 by Thomas Nelson. Used by permission. All rights reserved.
Scripture quotations taken from the Amplified® Bible (AMP), Copyright © 2015 by The Lockman Foundation. Used by permission. Lockman.org

ISBN 978-1-7393164-0-2 (Paperback)
ISBN 978-1-7393164-1-9 (eBook)
ISBN 978-1-7393164-2-6 (Audiobook)

Published by ProVision
www.provisioncreatives.com
Unit 69489
PO Box 6945
London
W1A 6US

printed in the United Kingdom

DISCERN THE TIME

DEDICATION

I dedicate this book to Josiah, Tobias, and Charis: You have walked through challenges that God alone knows.
My prayer is that you will learn to see that there has always been a greater design than what you may currently see in this present time. The heartaches experienced through life are threads in a larger tapestry woven into those of joy and laughter. This mother's longing is, not to spare you the pain, but that you will know Him more fully, which is gain.

"To the only God, our Saviour, through Jesus Christ our Lord, be glory, majesty, dominion, and authority, before all time and now and forever. Amen."

Jude 1:25

CONTENTS

FOREWORD

My wife and I have been in ministry and church leadership for more than thirty-five years. During this time, we have seen the importance and necessity of listening and hearing God's voice for His prophetic direction.

Alongside leadership, God raises up those who have a prophetic grace on their lives in order to confirm, encourage, strengthen and give further insight to the direction of what God is saying to His people. Coupled with this, will be the clarity of the response needed to see what He is saying being outworked and fulfilled.

Our friendship with Sarah goes back more than thirty-five years. Having initially met working together in ministry, Sarah was not only gifted in dance and creative arts but also prophetically. For many years, we have seen her grow and develop not only in her call and gifting, but also how she has sought to serve and invest in others along the way.

At the heart of Sarah's life has been a strong desire to know Jesus, to hear from Him and then do whatever He says, even when all the odds have been stacked against her. She has sought to live out what she is spurring us on to live, through what she writes in these pages.

God always speaks ahead of time to prepare the hearts and minds of His people, so they are not caught off guard by the events happening in the world, but instead are ahead of the curve knowing how to live in the face of all that is happening. Often He has to say the same thing in many different ways because we can be slow as His church to believe and respond to what He is saying.

The world runs on emotion. This is being fed by the continual stream of news, information and narratives through the various social and media platforms. So many voices are competing for our attention and affection aiming to direct us to a product, an opinion, a way of thinking and therefore a way of living. The intensity of the pressure to conform to the pattern and ways of this world are increasing day in and day out.

Therefore, in the midst of all that is happening, it is essential for the Christian to know The Voice in the noise to be able to Discern The Time to then be available and positioned for God's purposes.

Every believer can hear God's voice, the question is are we listening?

To make sure the church hears what He is saying, He speaks clearly to those who are listening, to then speak through them to His church.

'Discern The Time' is not simply a collection of prophetic words, but an unfolding revelation as to the time we are in and how we are to be as His church in this new era.

Each chapter needs personal reflection and response, to give time to align our hearts and minds to the lifestyle God is calling His church into. For some this might mean radical change, for others some simple adjustments. But whichever is relevant for you, I encourage you to listen to the Holy

Spirit as you read so that you Discern The Time and then position yourself for His purpose.

Clive Urquhart
Senior Pastor
Kingdom Faith Church

ACKNOWLEDGEMENTS

There are many names I could mention, but these are those who have helped shape me into the person I am today and without whom I could not have written this book.

My husband, Danny, you are my gift from Heaven, without whom this book would not exist. We have faced more storms than some on this earth, but from these, this book was born. Despite the battles, the victory is ours. Our story is one of perseverance and overcoming, daily, by His grace. Thank you for being here and for your encouragement to be faithful to the call on my life.

My precious mother, Beryl, you taught me how to praise through the darkness and sing in the rain. Your faith and dedication are an inspiration. Your silent sacrifices have been seen by God, and He will reward you in due season. Thank you for everything.

The following acknowledgements are to my three spiritual fathers, who have since been promoted to glory. I am forever grateful for the influence you had in my life and your tremendous passion for Jesus: **Mike Costello, Ray Goudie,** and **Colin Urquhart:**
Thank you for the shining example you were to me at different stages of my life. I didn't have an earthly father to show me the way, but I am so thankful that you demonstrated how to live for the One who is Life Himself.

An acknowledgement also goes to their respective *Proverbs 31* wives: **Pat,** who prayed with me that glorious first night I received the Lord. **Nancy,** who's been a dear friend and example to so many, faithfully serving Abba throughout her public ministry. And **Caroline,** a devoted woman of God who faithfully supported her husband so that he could travel the world with the message of God.

A Lesson for anyone wanting to write a book...

The story of the "Dear John" letter to my husband.

Have you ever written a "Dear John" letter? Usually, it's one of those breakup letters. Sadly, today, it's often done via text. Technically, I didn't write a breakup letter since my husband and I weren't even going out at the time. But he'd told me he was interested in me (on more than one occasion), and I wanted to make it blatantly clear that I wasn't! I sent him a letter, since he was living on the other side of the country at the time. The letter emphasised what I'd already told him, as I wasn't convinced he'd gotten the message. So I let him know that I didn't see any future for us together. However, to avoid sounding too harsh, I told him he was a great guy and prayed he'd find the *right* person. I wanted to encourage him to trust in the Lord, to lean not on his own understanding, but to acknowledge God in everything, knowing He'd direct his steps. Maybe you recognise those words from Scripture?

To communicate that sentiment, **I added the Bible verse at the end of my letter.**

On our honeymoon, my husband almost had the last laugh. But God had the final one, reminding us that He had been directing our steps all along.

My husband found the letter I'd written. He told me he'd asked a friend to look up the scripture at the bottom. "They never told me what it said," he commented, paging through his Bible. So I told him what it said.

Only it didn't.

I couldn't believe my mistake, as he read it aloud...

"She is more precious than rubies, nothing you desire can compare with her." *Proverbs 3:15 (NIV)*

I was dumbfounded. I'd written Proverbs 3:15 instead of Proverbs 3:5. That sneaky *"1"* completely changed the meaning of my letter. Instead of encouraging him, my letter insinuated - you can look, but you can't have.

Boy, did we laugh!

That little story aims to highlight the level of gratitude I have for those precious few who've helped me proofread and check my manuscript prior to publishing. There were many typos and places where I seemed to have a dose of word or number blindness. Thanks especially to **Michael, Kate,** and **Linda,** whose meticulous eye for detail and support mean this book should be as error-free as possible. If, however, you spot what we missed, please be gracious; maybe God wanted to speak something else to you :)

Last, but yet first, **my Lord and Saviour, Jesus Christ:** You promised never to leave or forsake me, and through it all, You have remained faithful to Your Word. Thank you for rescuing me from the pit of despair and strengthening me with grace to stand and persevere: to see the bigger picture. I am forever grateful for Your covenant of love.

"Do not be conformed to this world, but be transformed by the renewal of your mind, that by testing you may discern what is the will of God, what is good and acceptable and perfect."

Romans 12 v2 (ESV)

PREFACE

As summer turned to autumn in 2022, a sense of urgency arose in my spirit. All the words God had spoken to me over the previous seven years were swirling around my head; I couldn't rest until I laid them all out. I could hear the Father telling me to stop what I was doing, and write. And so this book was birthed.

It is a glimpse into what God has shown me. There is always more that could be said and more detail that could be unpacked. This may be a confirmation of what you have heard and seen in the Spirit, or it may be unknown to you and open up a whole new way of seeing. I acknowledge we see in part. My prayer is that whoever you are, and wherever you are on your spiritual walk, you may understand on a greater level the importance of the time we are living in.

This book aims to help and encourage you to **discern for yourself** what God is speaking, so that in the midst of numerous voices, you are not drawn by every wind of doctrine, *Ephesians 4:14*.

As you read this book, please receive it with the heart with which it was written. The aim is to encourage, build up, and help the Church to discern the time we are in.

May you find a fresh hunger for God's Word and be stirred to grow in your relationship with the One who is Love Himself: Father, Son, and Holy Spirit.

- ∞ Prophecy is passing and it is given in part.
- ∞ Love alone will never fail and it is love that must prevail.
- ∞ Take this offering of imperfection to hear for yourself the love that is Himself perfection.

> *"Love never fails. But where there are prophecies, they will cease; where there are tongues, they will be stilled; where there is knowledge, it will pass away. For we know in part and we prophesy in part, but when completeness comes, what is in part disappears."*

1 Corinthians 13:8-10 (NIV)

"And do this, understanding the present time: The hour has already come for you to wake up from your slumber, because our salvation is nearer now than when we first believed. The night is nearly over; the day is almost here. So let us put aside the deeds of darkness and put on the armour of light."

Romans 13 11-12 (NIV)

Let's Start Here

INTRODUCTION

Autumn (or fall, as my American friends say) is an interesting time. It is the beginning of the Jewish new year, yet the closing of ours. It is often a time of reflection: a time to look back over the year so far, as it heads towards a close, and think forward to the next. In October 2018, I was doing just that as I sat in Parliament, preparing to speak in the House of Commons. The documentary film I directed was being screened there to raise awareness of young suicide and mental health.

I reflected back to the film's premiere in March of that year. Little did the audience know, as they stood to their feet, cheering and applauding, as I declared life over death, what was going on behind the scenes. This was not a church-going audience; many had suffered loss through death by suicide. Yet, as I spoke **life** over the young people of our nation, they were unaware that the threat of death had just been delivered to my husband at the hospital. One month later, he was under the surgeon's knife, having emergency open heart surgery. This is the reality of living both a public and private life. It is often not what it appears to be. Whilst he was in surgery I knelt in prayer, surrendering my husband up to the Father. I thanked God for our life together, choosing to trust that He had both our futures in His hands. Our journey has not been easy, and we've faced many giants over the years, but the light shines brightest in the dark. Behind closed doors is where you are honed. It prepares you to be positioned and ready to step into your purpose.

What I've learned through those years is the importance of **discernment.** Why do bad things happen to God's people (or anyone)? How do you know if something is of God or the devil? How do you walk through the dark times? How do you know which voice to listen to?

How? By using discernment: to discern is to perceive or gain understanding of a situation, to recognise what is really going on. This is a time to have your eyes opened in order to **see from God's perspective**.

Walking through Parliament that day, following my film's screening, I was confronted with British history. Around me, statues of former leaders and decision-makers lined the halls and corridors. It hit me that the impact of those ruling choices has affected all of us in one way or another. Those parliamentarians left a legacy during their earthly time, for good or bad. My encouragement, as you read this book, is that you will aspire to leave an eternal legacy, to the glory of God.

This is the time we live in. You cannot change when you were born or the path God has set before you. But you can choose how to embrace the life you have.

- CHOOSE WISELY AND DISCERN

Sarah Holloway

1 ~

Chapter 1

DISCERN THE TIMES

During a short business conference in London, I visited an art gallery in Singapore. Large original pieces of art lined the gallery walls. Captivated by the detail of the art work, I was struck by one of the large portraits of a lion on display. I stepped back to admire the fine craftsmanship of the artist, who told me that as he laboured over every brush stroke, God had spoken to him about how He knows every hair on our heads.

I was transfixed as I walked around the gallery, admiring each intricate piece of art being exhibited. With only one other person in the gallery, it was easy to get lost in time, but I was aware of my need to return to the conference that I was attending in London. I took my Oculus headset off and handed it to someone else so that they could enter the world in Singapore that I'd just left.

God is on the move; it's time to wake up to the time that we're living in and hear what the Holy Spirit is saying.

Who could have thought that we would have tangible experiences in digital worlds back in the early 90s when the Web was launched? If you remember the time when we weren't reliant on mobile phones and smart devices, did you foresee a time when our lives would be dictated by internet connections? We stepped into a digital era unlike anything anyone could have imagined. Even Sir Tim Berners-Lee (who invented the Web) did not envisage the actual change that it has brought to the society we live in. Since the global 2020 lockdown, businesses and churches alike have sought to catch up with those who had already embraced the online space.

Love it or hate it, the Internet enables us to find connections. Whether that is via social media, virtual video calls, or other online spaces, we can now connect in an instant with others across the globe. Who could have guessed that business flights could turn into online conference meetings and remote working from home would become the ***norm***?

History is a great teacher.

When we stop to reflect on what's gone before, we start to see patterns that teach us important lessons. History is a great teacher that we can learn from. Take, for example, the media conglomerates that didn't discern the times. EMI had a rich British heritage as one of the major players in the music industry. It was the 4th largest record label in the world, following closely behind the 3 largest American ones. EMI owned Abbey Road Studios (made famous by the Beatles), EMI Records, Parlophone, Virgin Records, and Capitol Records. However, within a short period of time, it collapsed, having not recognised the importance of the digital age. Despite building a successful billion-pound media business, it missed the opportunity embraced by a couple of Swedish businessmen. The business partners, who had no background in music, identified a gap in the market following the closure of Napster (then an illegal music downloading site). They saw the opportunity to fill that gap and soon had the attention of the big guys, as their new venture quickly gained traction. The streaming service, Spotify, was taking the music industry by storm. Sadly, the wake-up call for EMI was too late. The record label faced huge financial losses and was forced to sell in 2012 to an American financial group before finally being bought out by the other *Big 3* conglomerates. Spotify's founders **discerned the times.**

This important lesson teaches us that if we stick to tradition and what we think we know, it's possible to lose sight of the opportunities ahead. Trends can inform us, but ultimately it is about recognising where the wind of the Spirit is blowing.

The Holy Spirit and the Word of God are where our compass should be anchored.

History can inform the future. So, as we look forward, we can reflect on what God is saying through the Bible, gain a clearer understanding of what lies ahead, and be aligned for future purpose - now.

> *"... The word of our God endures forever."*
> *Isaiah 40: 8*

As Christians, this should give us an advantage in discerning the time we are living in. But unfortunately, many Christian organisations appear to be following the trends set by others. Now is the time for the Church to arise and pioneer the way forward. There is no better time, as God is speaking

now. If we listen to His directing, then the world will have to sit up and take notice.

Are you ready to discern the times?

> *"And He changes times and the seasons;*
> *He deposes kings and raises up others;*
> *He gives wisdom to the wise*
> *And knowledge to the discerning.*
> *He reveals deep and hidden things;*
> *He knows what lies in darkness,*
> *And light dwells with Him."*
> *Daniel 2:21-22 (NIV)*

In the Book of Daniel, we read about how King Nebuchadnezzar was deeply troubled by a dream that none of his magicians or sorcerers could interpret. The content of the dream contained a clear message from God that wasn't only relevant for Nebuchadnezzar but also a prophetic statement relating to the future kingdoms and an acknowledgement of the One True God, *Daniel 2*.

Similarly, when Pharaoh was ruling over Egypt, he was disturbed by dreams. Joseph was brought out of prison to give him the interpretation, having interpreted dreams before. He sought the Lord as to the meaning of Pharaoh's dream, and God revealed it to him during the night. The warning of the famine and strategic positioning of Joseph resulted in the Israelites' survival, *Genesis 41*.

We're living in a time of the prophetic. *Joel 2* speaks of visions and dreams. So, we should not ignore them since the Lord speaks through them. Like with Joseph and Pharaoh, if we listen to what God is speaking and take the warnings seriously, then we can be prepared for what's coming.

What I'm about to share is to help you discern the time and prepare accordingly.

That means taking positive action, whatever that looks like for you. However, we need to know how to **discern that which is of God,** as opposed to what just sounds good to our itching ears, *2 Timothy 2:4-3.*

How do you discern?

By the Spirit of God and His Word, the Bible. This is your anchor. *1 John 4* states that you need to test the spirits to see if they are from God. John explains that you can identify this by recognising God's Spirit, who is full of love, and confessing Jesus as Lord. If a message is contrary to the Word of God, you will know that isn't God speaking. If you have been born again by the Holy Spirit, then the Spirit of God who lives inside you will also bear witness in your spirit.

I'm not one to usually have prophetic dreams, but recently I had a vivid dream that played on my mind. I awoke with a keen sense that what I'd just seen in my dream was significant. I recorded the details and shared them with my pastor. In essence, I saw the keys of the Church being snatched out of a young woman's hand. She'd been given the keys by the owner of the church, but quite suddenly a motorbike appeared behind her without warning and the rider took them from her.

The message I believe God was conveying to me is that the Church must not become complacent at this time. We need to be vigilant, keep hold of what God has entrusted to us, and protect it wisely.

"Be alert and of sober mind. Your enemy

*the devil prowls around like a roaring lion
looking for someone to devour."
1 Peter 5:8 (NIV)*

My prayer is that, as you read this, you will indeed discern the times and understand your role within God's divine plan.

Please note before you begin...

This book is not just to be read and put on your shelf. It is one that seeks to motivate you and stir a response within you. My hope is that your love relationship with God will be awakened, rekindled, or increased as you allow the Holy Spirit to speak to you through the offerings within the pages.

Within the pages there are multiple references to scripture, and whether these are new or known to you, my prayer is that you will find fresh revelations and whispers from above. To help with this, there is space at the end of each section where you can journal your own thoughts and reflections, write down any key Bible verses that speak to you, or your own prayer response.

JOURNAL YOUR THOUGHTS

Space to reflect and respond to the Holy Spirit

Use the space after each chapter to write, doodle, or draw your own thoughts, reflections, meditations, or prayer.

BIBLE  Make note of any key Scripture

Write your prayer to God **PRAYER**

"I am your servant; give me discernment that I may understand your statutes."

Psalm 119: 125

If you do not know what to pray, I encourage you to read aloud the prayer the Lord Himself taught you to pray. As you do, allow the words to connect with your heart and mind.

"And when you pray, do not use vain repetitions as the heathen do. For they think that they will be heard for their many words.
"Therefore do not be like them. For your Father knows the things you have need of before you ask Him. In this manner, therefore, pray:
Our Father in heaven
Hallowed be Your name.
Your kingdom come.
Your will be done
On earth as it is in heaven.
Give us this day our daily bread.
And forgive us our debts,
As we forgive our debtors.
And do not lead us into temptation,
But deliver us from the evil one.
For Yours is the kingdom and the power and the glory forever. Amen."*

Matthew 6:7-13 (NKJV)

*Note verse 13 is omitted from some versions, but is present in the original Greek and ancient versions of scripture. I personally think it is good to affirm God's Lordship and reign over our lives and the earth, when we pray.

2 ~

Chapter 2

A NEW DISPENSATION

It seems that there are times in my life when God literally steps in. These aren't times that I can predict or usher in. I am unable to summon the Lord at my own request. Yes, the reality is that when we quieten our spirits before Him, He will speak. Yet, there are also times of silence, when the Father is calling us into a deeper level of faith and trust. But what I am referring to here, are the moments when God has a greater purpose in revealing some sort of revelation or movement of His Spirit. Why does He use me? I do not know, other than He uses earthen vessels from which to pour out a richer treasure that is within; that of Himself.

> *"Now we have this treasure in jars of*
> *clay to show that this surpassingly great*
> *power is from God and not from us."*
> *2 Corinthians 4:7 (NIV)*

The first time I experienced an instance like this was about one year after giving my life to Jesus at a little obscure church, having not even heard the sermon. God literally took me from obscurity and positioned me in that year. Where nobody saw and nobody knew He was working in my heart, teaching and preparing me for what He had already planned. It was then that I encountered what I can only describe as a heavy download and awareness of the Holy Spirit about to move. Within about three months of carrying this perception, God revealed His plan. I found myself taken from obscurity and put on a stage in front of thousands of people in Jönköping. Seated on the front row was the King and Queen of Sweden. There, on that stage, I shared the Gospel and performed, as it was aired live on national Swedish television.

However, did you know that God has a sense of humour? Part way through my debut public speech in front of royalty, the entire auditorium erupted with laughter. The sniggering King and Queen even had me flummoxed. Not until I'd returned to my host's home did I find out what I'd done! Keep reading until the end and I'll let you in on what happened later - it's a pretty awesome testimony, but I don't want to digress.

Little did I realise back then, aged twenty, that I had been given a voice to communicate God's heart. Since that time the Lord has awakened me to many pre-empting moments like this. The words and downloads are not just about me, they are for you. They are for a specific period in time - This is one such time.

Some years ago, God impressed a word in my spirit. I had no idea what it meant, but this word I'm about to share, about **a new dispensation**, came to me so strongly that I had to stop everything to write it down. It is the focal point or anchor to everything else that I will share with you. I have received much revelation and fresh vision, but this word helps to put the other insights into greater context. Although each chapter and morsel could be taken on their own, they are more powerful when tethered to this word. I encourage you to take time to meditate on the truths within the scripture references, and allow the Holy Spirit to illuminate His living Word to you, so that you can apply it in your life.

This is the vision and the word that God gave me in January 2019

A New Dispensation

Seasons come and go. This is a new era, a new time - an epoch that has never been before and will not be again. A period of unfavoured and unmerited grace like never before. An outpouring of the Spirit beyond Acts. A time of preparation of the new wineskins for the new wine.

What is the definition or biblical meaning of **dispensation**?

"A certain order, system, or arrangement; administration or management."

Theology:
1. the divine ordering of the affairs of the world.
2. an appointment, arrangement, or favour, as by God.
3. a divinely appointed order or age.

4. the old Mosaic, or Jewish, dispensation; the new gospel, or Christian, dispensation.

> *"...having made known to us the mystery of His will, according to His good pleasure which He purposed in Himself, that in the **dispensation of the fullness of the times** He might gather together in one all things in Christ, both which are in heaven and which are on earth—in Him."*
> *Ephesians 1:9-10 (NKJV)*

> *"The voice of one crying in the wilderness: 'Prepare the way of the Lord; Make straight in the desert A highway for our God. Every valley shall be exalted. And every mountain and hill brought low; The crooked places shall be made straight And the rough places smooth; The glory of the Lord shall be revealed, And all flesh shall see it together; For the mouth of the Lord has spoken.'"*
> *Isaiah 40:3-5 (NKJV)*

Many prophecies are talking of a new season, but a few months ago God spoke to me, that not so much is a new season upon us, but the word He spoke was, that the shift is into **a new dispensation** (though I had never heard this word before). The Holy Spirit showed me that seasons come and go, they ebb and flow, they turn and repeat, but this time is not one that has been before, and it is not one that will be repeated. The time is of the age. It is a time that the Spirit has been eagerly awaiting, for a time such as now, a new period of dispensation, which will require a new level of stewardship. One that will require the Church to move as a united body to reap the harvest...

This period will be unlike anything that the Church has known before. What has gone before was a glimpse and a preparation for this time. This dispensation is unlike any era that has been. *Isaiah 43:18.* I felt God say that as we enter into this new period of time that is being ushered in, ensure that there is no unfinished business, no outstanding debt of forgiveness or unconfessed sin.

> *"Anyone you forgive, I also forgive.*
> *And what I have forgiven—if there*
> *was anything to forgive—I have*
> *forgiven in the sight of Christ for*
> *your sake, in order that Satan*
> *might not outwit us. For we are not*
> *unaware of his schemes."*
> *2 Corinthians 2: 10-11 (NIV)*

Be alert to instruction in the Word. (Read and note what you are shown in *Ephesians 4:25-32*). Attend to that which the Lord shows you in order that anything that could be a thread to the past is cut, so that you can receive the fullness of this dispensation, to move freely into everything the Lord has without hindrance. Let your hands open fully to receive, as they let go of what has gone before. Letting go, not just the pain and wrestle of previous years, but letting go of the good, of the accolade, the rewards, and even the fruit, which is all His and all to His Glory. *2 Timothy 1:9 ; Isaiah 48:11.* Nothing you had before should you bring into the new, except the wisdom and the anointing that God has been growing in you through the developing of your character, by the Spirit of God. *Romans 5:3-4 ;Matthew 9:17.*

God has been renewing the mindset of His people and transforming them, in preparation for this dispensation.

This dispensation is one of the Spirit. There will be a move and an outpouring of the Spirit that will rest upon those who have availed themselves. There will be a special grace that is given, a dispensation of unmerited grace and favour to fulfil the call. *Titus 2:11-15.* For this is the time of the harvest and all the labourers should join together, a connected body, united in its purpose. *John 17:23.* The Church cannot presuppose how the Spirit will move, but God is downloading the strategy, the blueprint, so that each will know how to position themselves and step out into the call, *I Chronicles 28:19*

However, God would call us to be vigilant and alert. *1 Peter 5:8.* The enemy is a defeated foe, but as the nations become spiritually awake, so the deceiver will continue to try and deceive even the elect. *Matthew 24:24 James 4:7.* Discernment is the gift you should seek, as you continue to glorify the King of Kings and Lord of Lords. Praise is the gateway to victory. The Word is your sword; it will give you clarity to discern what is true, *Hebrews 4:12,* to discern between flesh and Spirit, and between spirits. *1 John 4:1.* Meditate on the Word of God.

Read it, chew on it, speak it, recite and sing it, declare it. For My Word is at work. *Isaiah 55:11*

Allow your spirit to be open to the Word in a fresh way, allow the Holy One to open your eyes to truths you have not seen before, for this is a time of greater depth of revelation, and you will perceive things that were previously hidden. *Psalm 119: 97-100* So, seek out the hidden treasures in the Word, re-read and absorb what you thought you already knew, but had not seen before, within the sanctum∗. *Daniel 2:22, Jeremiah 33:3*

[∗sanctum: a sacred or holy place - a private place]

The Word will not only protect you, but also equip you to open blind eyes and quicken the spirit within a person. The Word, in this dispensation, is imperative. By it, you will be like a scalpel in the Lord's hand that can cut to the heart with precision, as you speak truth. *Isaiah 49:2*. So be excited, get prepared, acquire the strategy, be built up in the Word and walk with discernment into the dispensation that's before us. To be joined together to see the harvest brought in, before the return of the King. *Revelation 14:15*

A new dispensation is the Word God spoke to me several years ago, but one that continues to echo loudly in my spirit and I will anchor back to it in conjunction with the rest of this book. Some people kept saying, "I can't wait to get back to normal". Even before the second lockdown, I remember saying to my husband, "we're headed for a *new normal.*" I knew there was more to come because God had said that He was allowing a shaking of the natural things to break open, re-order and align to the spiritual in a new way.

As we continue to transition to the new dispensation, you need to be aligned to God's Word, prepared for what is ahead and built up in Him who is Truth. Then you will live in the grace to walk in step with God. Like Noah, that may mean stepping out in radical obedience (note here, not wacky or piously zealous, but in surrender to the God of Love, so that His Love may be revealed). That means, like Noah, sometimes going against the grain of what makes sense in our natural understanding.

To discern is to recognise the bigger picture and see the hand of God at work. It's the ability to separate the parts (of life) and see how they each connect. In other words, having discernment means you understand what is really happening in that moment. You perceive what is of the Spirit in comparison to what is of the flesh or natural world; you recognise the difference between the Spirit of God and the spirits of this world. You identify the motives and thoughts of the human heart, so that you can see clearer the intent of God.

As communities we have all suffered some major losses. We should join together in comforting those who mourn. But it is also important to see from a more global perspective what has been taking place. A generation has been taken. Many generals of the faith have been promoted to glory. These were the spiritual leaders for a generation. It was their time. That, however, has an impact on those of us who have been left behind. We need to mourn our loss, but also to rise above as we celebrate their lives, by living ours in surrender to the God of Glory who has your/our name(s) written in the Lamb's book of life, *Revelation 21:27.*

> *"Comfort, comfort my people, says your*
> *God. Speak tenderly to Jerusalem, and*
> *proclaim to her that her hard service has*
> *been completed..."*
> *Isaiah 40: 1-2 (NIV)*

Οἰκονομία is the Greek word for dispensation, which means office of administration or stewardship. We are each stewards of the Gospel. This is a time where God is entrusting us to steward and administer what He is revealing to the Church. This book will unpack much of what it is that God is reordering so that you can discern what you are being called to oversee and steward. Then you will be prepared and positioned for what lies ahead.

Let me take you through a journey of fresh discovery and renewed hunger for the things of God.

JOURNAL YOUR THOUGHTS

BIBLE

PRAYER

3 ~

Chapter 3

TIME

The online age and the knock-on effect of situations such as lockdown, have ushered in a new era of digital connection. I'm sure, like me, your life has been impacted with online meetings in some form or another. Many churches now stream virtually in addition to meeting in person. For me, coaching and connecting with people around the world across different time zones is an interesting experience. No longer am I restricted to set working hours. Congregating together across nations means I need to be flexible with my time. Sitting in a meeting with people who are watching the sun rise, whilst others have the sunset behind their window at the same time, is awesome. Connecting with a group of people meeting at different times of the day, all at the *same time!*

Just as with my little analogy, there are times that **look different for each of us and a time that is the same for everyone.** We can meet at different times around the world, in the very same moment of time.

49

God created time.

> *"God called the light Day, and the darkness He*
> *called Night. So the evening and the morning*
> *were the first day. "*
> *Genesis 1:5 (NIV)*

As you read through *Genesis 1:14-19* you can see how God created the ability for us to measure time, setting the sun, moon and stars in the sky to serve as signs to mark sacred times, days and years. God declared it good. Time should perhaps, therefore, be our friend. However, it can often work against us. We talk about being early, late, or on time. You may try to 'beat the clock' or 'race against time', but ultimately it is good to remember, our times are in God's hands *Psalm 31: 15*.

The Bible uses many words that have been translated as time. But this form of linear time is identified with the Greek word **chronos**, from which derives the term chronological. Chronos may refer to a literal period of or moment in time. Most of us have been governed by this type of time, (in the sense of our waking, working, sleeping hours), and our schedules generally align to it. We have set up our own structures within this framework set by God, that is man-made. I am not saying it is good or bad, but am just stating how it is. Some people keep to a rigid time frame, whilst others have a more leisurely view towards time, all for their own reasons that can be both positive and negative.

You may have already noticed that this book is entitled with the use of **time** (singular), whereas the chapter of the same name uses **times** (plural). Throughout this book, I use the words, time and times. It may appear that I interchangeably use the word in both the singular and plural. Although there are instances when either can be used quite acceptably, there are moments where it is helpful to understand why I have used the singular over the plural or vice versa.

In addition to chronos time, there are two other key words used in Scriptures to define time. In the Old Testament the Hebrew word **moed**. This means an **appointed time**; a fixed moment. This can relate to a set festival, for example. In the Book of *Daniel*, this term is used several times, specifically in *chapter 11*. Daniel speaks prophetically about an appointed time that is coming, in relation to what most would define as the end times.

> *"...until the time of the end, for it will still come **at the appointed time.***"
> *Daniel 11:35 (NIV)*

When God impressed on me the word about a new dispensation, I would describe it as **an appointed time**. Note, therefore, that I have used the word, time, in its singular form. We are entering and living in a specific time; a set time. This is a corporate time within which we have entered, and are all entering.

Additionally, there are times, which are more like seasons within which we all live. Our seasons may vary and be different from each other. For example, when children are born or leave home, parents may enter a new season of life. Raising the child(ren) is for a period of time that may not be the same for someone else. A mother may give up her career to stay at home to nurse her baby, whereas the father may continue in his job. The arrival of a baby will have entered them both into a new period of time. Yet the times are different for each. Hence why it is important to recognise this time, this new dispensation and be able to discern your place in it.

Kairos, is a Greek word used in the New Testament for time. Kairos defines an opportune time, or appropriate moment. Jesus uses this word when He talks about **discerning the time**.

> *"...how is it ye do not **discern this time?**"*
> *Luke 12:56 KJV*

Imagine farmers preparing to harvest their crops. Then harvest time arrives. If the weather is unsatisfactory the farmers will no doubt delay reaping their fields until the weather is good. However, the location and weather for one group of farmers may be different to another's. One group may have been able to gather in the crops because the storms hadn't yet reached them. It is harvest time for both - and both harvest their crops during this time. And yet, each may have harvested them at a different time, i.e. on a different day during harvest time.

Hopefully, this little allegory helps to explain how the Kairos moment of time we are in demands you to discern. We have entered and are entering a time that is an opportune moment. Just like the exact moment of harvest that may not be the same time for you as someone else. And yet this is a *Kairos* moment we are living in: The right or **opportune moment** in which God is calling you and I to awake, see, be alert and discern.

It is God who orders your time and directs your steps and who knows that you are called, "... **for such a time as this**'. *Esther 4:14*

JOURNAL YOUR THOUGHTS

BIBLE

PRAYER

4 ~

Chapter 4

CROSSROADS

A drive through the countryside is something I thoroughly enjoy. I love exploring and capturing those unique moments of nature, being able to soak in God's creation, whilst never knowing quite where you're going to end up. However, when I used to be on tour, driving through those country lanes was something of a challenge. In the days before sat navs and mobile phones, I could find myself lost in the middle of nowhere. I would search for signposts at each junction. Yet sometimes they were absent, broken, or moved. Even if there was a signpost, quite often the names of the villages on them meant nothing to me. Somehow, they didn't all make their way into my map and I'd find myself off the page. If you remember navigating with one of those little map books, you'll know what I mean!

Back then, garages were fewer and didn't open 24/7, so travelling home after a gig the other side of the country meant I couldn't afford to get off route. I needed an internal navigational system. There were times when God literally guided me through the night hours along endless country lanes with hardly any fuel in the tank. That example is just one of how I've had to learn to rely on the inner still small voice (of God). I hope this chapter helps you to **discern that voice.**

Since 2021 I have coached numerous individuals around the world. They have come from an array of different backgrounds, of all ages, and in unconnected situations. Yet interestingly, each person I've met appears to be facing a pivotal moment in their life. Do you recognise this transitional space we are in?

Are you at a point of change of direction in your own life?

I wrote the word about *a new dispensation* in January 2019, prior to lockdown, sensing a major shift was about to take place. Looking back, we can see how the disruption of lockdown due to Covid-19, pushed society out of its *normal* state and escalated us into a new equilibrium. However, I believe that we are still in a transition and the following vision below, I received one year earlier. It is applicable to everyone in this period, and on reflection, easier to put this vision into context.

It is time to recognise what God is speaking to the Church, and specifically to you individually. There is much turmoil, confusion, and overwhelm in the lives of many Christians at this time. Much of that is because people cannot see clearly. There are many crossroads or junctions in their lives, but this is the valley of decision. *Joel 3:14*

Although I wrote the following vision down some time ago, only now are we experiencing the manifestation of what I saw. I believe that we, both as individuals and as the Church, are currently facing a crossroads.

This is the vision and the word that God gave me in 2018
(please note, I will explain more about 'the sound' later)

The Crossroads

Many are hearing that God is speaking about a shift, a change, a new wine for new wine skins, but there are few who know what this means.

> *I saw a vision of a multitude ready to move, but they were at a crossroads; facing a junction that seemed impossible. Similar to the children of Israel seemingly stranded on the banks of the Red Sea, these people were God's people who had faithfully travelled a journey out of bondage and slavery having travelled through hardship and struggle now looking for the Promised Land. So too, they were now at a juncture facing the unknown. Others were slowly catching them up and together they were becoming a force to be reckoned with, but they didn't know it yet. (An army of ordinary people are rising).*

Whilst I continued to look, the waters parted and those who heard the sound stepped out in faith, trusting the leading of the Spirit. But those who were still enslaved in their thinking to the old were fearful and reasoned with their own logic. Some looked for an alternative route, a way around or a short cut; others turned back; but many just sat watching those who were going. For some apathy, and others anxious fear, held them back from advancing into the unknown. And still others had prideful rebellion that led to independence, believing they knew a better way, wanting people to follow them. However, some quickly followed after those who were stepping out when they suddenly realised they were about to be left behind.

As the waters separated and dry land appeared, or light lit the way at the crossroads, a vast crowd stepped forward into the unknown. And almost it seemed, in an instant, the way disappeared from view. At the crossroads the path was no longer lit up, and the waves again covered the dry land again. The multitude that had journeyed on was no longer in sight; the way was closed up and could not be found. Many were left stranded on the bank or still at the crossroads unable to find the way.

God is sending a warning: do not miss the turning of the tide, the changing of the track, or the changing of the season. Recognise the signs, hear the sound, and follow the leading of the His Spirit who is creating a new wineskin for new wine.

In preparation there is a 'shift' taking place that is aligning God's body like an arrow being drawn and getting ready to fire. Every feather in the quiver is joined to the shaft in alignment to be fired according to the direction of the wind, in order for the arrow to hit the mark. So too, it is time to connect and join with the other members to become one body that moves in unity with every part fulfilling its intended purpose, as the Holy Spirit directs.

Standing at the junction, what you see before you will look different to what you have known; it is not something you have seen before. It will not sound, taste, smell, or even feel the same as what you have heard, tasted, smelled, or touched before. **What is before you and what is coming is not something you have ever experienced before.** You will not recognise it because of what you have previously known or understood. Nor will you know it by what you have been taught; you will not know it, except by the Holy Spirit.

There is a sound, those who are listening hear it; those who have aligned themselves are the ones who are listening. Others are starting to listen and beginning to hear. There will also be a smell, an aroma that won't be like anything that has been breathed before. It will be the fragrance of the Spirit coming from those who, together, move at the sound of the call. As they march in advancement their trail will beckon others to join them. Some will be drawn by their perfume, but others will be repelled (those with prideful rebellion in their hearts).

It calls for a submissive heart, open to the Holy Spirit; a warrior spirit that puts aside the weariness from the fight, to receive a refreshing from the dew and rain that the Lord is giving in this season. There must be a love, not only for the Saviour Himself, but also for one another. This is not a time for holding regrets or grudges against others, or yourself. It is not a time for gazing back as Lot's wife did when she turned into a pillar of salt, but it is a time for looking forward. It is a time of preparing, of aligning with God and each other, as the Spirit assigns each to their position. Do not judge by your own understanding, and do not judge your brother or sister by their call. It will not look like the old and without the Holy Spirit will not make sense to your natural mind, but you will know those who are His by the mark of the Holy Spirit. During this time of positioning, do not look to the old ways, to the old wineskin that is being discarded, but allow your mind to be renewed and as you clothe yourself with the mind of Christ, you will begin to have insight like never before. Do not delay until the things you are waiting for have changed. Whether married or single, young or old, male or female, rich or poor, no matter your circumstance, culture or background, it is time to prepare. Prepare as the Israelites did in Egypt before Passover, ready for the sound, on stand-by until it is time to advance and move out. *Exodus 12*

Right now, some are standing ready with their sandals tied, their water bottles filled, and their swords sharpened. Others have noticed and are tying their laces and preparing to go, but some are just sitting enjoying the scenery, and others disgruntled are turning back. Don't judge what others are doing to prepare, do what God lays on your heart to do, but don't go back to the familiar patterns and ways of learnt behaviour and mind-sets. Do not let the former things hold you back. Do not dwell on the sins, rejection, abuse, fear, failure, or anything else that has previously held you back. Allow God to heal and move you beyond them.

Instead, seek the ancient paths *Jeremiah 6:16*. Seek the truth whilst He may be found, seek His face and follow His lead. Your family, your jobs, your dreams, your call will see a touch from the Holy One as you seek His face.

Don't misjudge the timing.

Now as I re-read this word myself, I am in awe of how God was clearly speaking to me back in 2018, warning of what was to come. But we are just at the beginning. I encourage you to soak in what the Lord would show you through this word, as there is a rich instruction that will help you move forward in this time. My hope is that it will open your spiritual eyes to what has and is happening, so that you are equipped and prepared for what is still to come.

God gives us signposts and this book may be one for you right now. There is a way that may seem hard, but it is the one that many others before you have travelled. 'The ancient paths' is what the Lord is speaking in this time. There you will find rest. You will know a deep sense of peace and wellbeing as you walk along these paths.

*"This is what the Lord says: 'Stand at
the crossroads and look; ask for the
ancient paths, ask where the good way is,
and walk in it, and you will find rest for
your souls.'"*
Jeremiah 6:16 (NIV)

The prophet Jeremiah's plea from the Lord to the children of Israel was to follow the ancient paths. To not lose sight of the directions they had learnt from Abraham and Moses. The path that the apostles encouraged the early Church to follow. The Israelites, however, forgot to stick to the paths and were drawn away by other religions and idols. There were consequences to their actions, not in the least that they missed out on the blessings of health, peace, abundance, security, and knowing the presence of God. *Ezekiel 34: 25-31.* Although God, in His mercy made a way for them to return, by taking the punishment they deserved on Himself, through the crucifixion of Jesus. It is a reminder for us not to take anything for granted. Many of the Jews have still not received the blessing through Christ, God wants to remind you that you can receive all that He has bought for you on that cross. It is time to discern the path.

We are surrounded by so many voices at this time, telling us which way to go that it can be difficult to know which one to follow. So, I'll be sharing some more navigational tips in another chapter, in order to help you read the signs and discern how to follow the right ones.

JOURNAL YOUR THOUGHTS

BIBLE

PRAYER

5 ~

Chapter 5

THE ARK

This is what God started to reveal in January 2020

I couldn't escape that nagging feeling. It was December when I read an article about a half size model of Noah's Ark that had arrived in the UK. Something inside me knew I needed to go and see it. Eventually a few weeks later, in January 2020, I travelled to Ipswich where it was docked.

The Dutch built floating Ark Museum covered 2,000 metres over 4 floors with impressive wooden sculptures representing biblical stories. However, as much as I admired all the painstaking work that had gone into this artwork, I was struck more by the sense of God speaking to me through the Ark itself.

Over the coming weeks, I knew that the Holy Spirit was impressing a sense of importance surrounding the Ark. You can read about Noah's journey in *Genesis chapters 6 - 9* about how the world was full of wickedness and God chose

Noah who walked blameless in his generation, to rescue humankind. The Bible doesn't inform us about where Noah lived or how the people around him responded to him building this massive structure. It has been speculated that he dwelt in Mesopotamia, which is modern day Iraq. But wherever it was, we can surmise that building a large vessel to float on water certainly wouldn't have made sense to the natural mind, since the land is mainly desert. Noah heard from God and obeyed, by faith.

> *"By faith Noah, when warned about things not yet seen, in holy fear built an ark to save his family. By faith he condemned the world and became heir of the righteousness that is in keeping with faith."*
> *Hebrews 11:7 (NIV)*

Visiting this awesome structure certainly led me to contemplate some of these things and to re-read the story of the flood, whilst listening to hear what the Lord was speaking.

Radical faith and being prepared was the first thing that God laid in my spirit.

Are you ready for the unexpected?

Did the Covid lockdowns throw you off guard?

We've all heard about numerous businesses going into liquidation or losing huge investments because they weren't expecting the shift. After receiving the download about a new dispensation, I told a few close to me that we needed to be prepared for a seismic shift, because something was coming. I could never have foreseen what it was, but when

Covid hit and the lockdown was announced, I wasn't surprised. I felt a sense of anticipation.

Now don't get me wrong... I was hit by the challenges personally in different ways that were painful and difficult. Many people lost loved ones, jobs, and the stability they had known before, and we cannot underestimate the pain and suffering this has caused many. But despite the challenges and sense of deep loss all around, I was expectant because God had been preparing me in my spirit. The words He had already spoken to me were now unravelling before me.

Isaiah 40 has been a scripture that has been strong in my spirit for some time. It calls out about our purpose to prepare the way of the Lord and reminds us that our destiny is one of eternal blessings. As we fix our eyes above the temporal, we can begin to see a great light of hope for what is awaiting us in eternity. Our life on earth is short, but we have a victory that is certain when we surrender our lives to Our Saviour.

> *"...All people are like grass, and all their faithfulness is like the flowers of the field. The grass withers and the flowers fall, because the breath of the Lord blows on them. Surely the people are grass. The grass withers and the flowers fall, but the word of our God endures forever."*
> *Isaiah 40: 6-8 (NIV)*

The second thing that struck me profoundly after visiting the ark, was that it is time to build an ark. The ark represents a vessel of salvation. A place where Noah, his family, and each kind of animal could be rescued from the impending flood.

I sensed a metaphorical **flood** was imminent and the Holy Spirit impressed on my heart the need to prepare something that would be able to rescue those who were drowning. Does your heart cry like mine for those devoid of hope who seek to find a reason to live? There are so many people empty and lost, wandering aimlessly through life wanting to be rescued. I believe we are called to build **arks** that will offer hope and healing. That will look different for each one of us. We are all part of a body and we are not to judge what we do not understand. So let the different parts build, as they are led by God. Ultimately, we are all smaller parts of a much larger vision: God building His Church.

You may be questioning what these arks will look like? How are we to build? What is your part in this? What it looks like for different people may not be the same, but there shall be similarities because God is laying out the blueprint.

I will unpack more regarding these questions in later chapters, and and explain what God has shown me these will look like, so that you can consider your part in building these arks. For now, add your own reflections, before we continue on this journey of adventure together...

JOURNAL YOUR THOUGHTS

BIBLE

PRAYER

6 ~

30 Cubits   50 Cubits

Chapter 6

THE BLUEPRINT

The next thing God spoke to me clearly after visiting the Ark was **blueprint**. Whilst I continued to meditate on the Bible verses surrounding the story of the ark, I was unable to *do* little else. I've carried much vision in my heart for what I believe God wants me to help build for more years that I can remember. I thought this must be my point of releasing the vision, but all I could get was a deep impression in my spirit that I needed to **sit and wait**.

However, this waiting was not a *do nothing*, but an active waiting on the Lord. I was continually turning inward, within my mind and inner being, to connect with the Holy Spirit, even whilst I went about my daily activities. It was as if God was downloading something heavy into my spirit. All around me I could see others starting to build. The opportunity of the new found online world was engaging everyone and sparking fresh ideas and dreams were being awakened to possibility. But God was urging me to wait.

Through this period, I was drawn to delve more into the Word. Whilst still carrying the weight of the prophetic nature of the Ark, I turned to *Genesis 6*. Reading through the Scriptures I could clearly see that Noah was given **the blueprint** for the Ark.

> *"So make yourself an ark of*
> *cypress wood; make rooms in it and*
> *coat it with pitch inside and out.*
> ***This is how you are to build it:***
> *The ark is to be three hundred cubits long,*
> *fifty cubits wide and thirty cubits high.*
> *Make a roof for it, leaving below the roof*
> *an opening one cubit high all around. Put a*
> *door in the side of the ark and make lower,*
> *middle and upper decks."*
> *Genesis 6:14-16 (NIV)*

God gave specific instruction to Noah telling him how he should build. The design, materials, and measurements were all detailed. He didn't just provide an idea or a concept. No, God was precise in His plan of action. Additionally, there was a strategic timing about the story of Noah. Dates and times are clearly evident throughout the Bible, demonstrating to us that these are significant. This is a prompting of the Spirit. It is vital that you do not run ahead of God's timing with your own agenda. We are called to sit at His feet to hear what the Spirit is speaking through His Word to us. The Bible is God's Word to us. It is our plumbline and our anchor. God will show you the way and guide you into all truth to bring you into the fullness of life, *John 16:13*.

> *"Jesus answered, 'I am the way and the*
> *truth and the life. No one comes to the*

Father except through me.'"
John 14:6 (NIV)

This is the time to hear God, receive the download, and walk yoked with the Holy Spirit, so you can keep in step. He will enable you to discern the big picture, without missing the detail, if you keep aligned in this way.

Let me tell you a story that contains an interesting parable.

My husband and I were locked in battle. Hunched over my kitchen table, I was intent that he wasn't going to win this fight. I could almost hear the chink of the sword being drawn and the horses' hooves, as my knight counter attacked on the chess board. He was not going to steal my queen this game, she had her faithful defender mounted to the rescue. This time my queen was safe! Only she wasn't. Well, technically my queen was no longer in danger, I'd seen to that, but the next move was checkmate!! How did that happen? I'd lost sight of what was important. Whether you play or not, I'm sure you know the aim is to capture the king, not the queen.

However, this was the distraction that lost me the game. I was so intent on saving my queen because I thought it was the most important piece. My husband had cleverly distracted my attention away from a seemingly insignificant piece that was slowly and steadily working its way up the board to corner my king. He was able to use this distraction of attacking my queen to cloak his intention, using the humble pawn to accomplish the winning checkmate move.

Chess is a great game of strategy. I am not an expert chess player, but I have learnt much through playing the game.

Not least, how to recognise the enemy's tactics, in addition to how we may respond, whether passively, on the attack or in defence. This lesson teaches it is vital to have your eyes on the real goal. I encourage you to pause and reflect on what has your focus. Is what's capturing your attention, like my queen, something of seeming importance, but not the ultimate prize?

Our enemy doesn't play fair, he is sneaky. If your focus is misdirected, you could miss the purpose in that moment. It is so important to have your eyes open and your heart soft to the Lord. This is why you must be reliant on the Holy Spirit and not leaning on your own understanding. *Proverbs 3:5.* When my children were younger learning to play chess, I found it difficult not to interfere. Sitting on the side-lines watching them play my husband, I'd find myself trying to catch their eye and direct them to a piece on the board with my eye. If they saw where I was staring, they could quickly see where the danger was coming from, or where there was an opportunity in front of them.

This is how God directs us.... with His eye.

> *"I will instruct you and teach*
> *you in the way you should go;*
> ***I will guide you with My eye.****"*
> *Psalm 32:8 (NKJV)*

Note here I've quoted the NKJ version (from the KJV), which is one of the few Bible versions that uses the term, **with My eye**. God spoke clearly to me, as I searched the original Hebrew to see if the interpretation was different. The Holy Spirit beautifully unpacked the chess scenario to me. As a Father watches over us, He lovingly directs us with His eye.

'Ê·nî. with My eye
ayin: an eye
Original Word: עֵין

Just as I directed my children with my eye. This is how, as the verse says, He instructs and teaches you the way you should go. Unfortunately, my chess directing was not always the best guidance, as I am not a chess master. But the Father is the best Life Master anyone could have. He has the master blueprint for our lives and, just like with Noah, God will give you the instructions.

Since hearing the word, **blueprint**, I now see it everywhere. It is as if it has become the *in thing.* Everyone appears to be offering their form of blueprint. Many are good and given from the Lord, but I encourage you to lean into Him, to hear for yourself where He wants to direct you. What I see in the spirit is a download of both individual and corporate blueprints being distributed from above. This will include businesses and ministries (though all is our ministry in the Lord) that have a unique blueprint design. New strategies and impartations of design and planning are being distributed from above. But in order to adapt to these God ordained initiatives, there needs to be new vessels.

JOURNAL YOUR THOUGHTS

BIBLE

PRAYER

7 ~

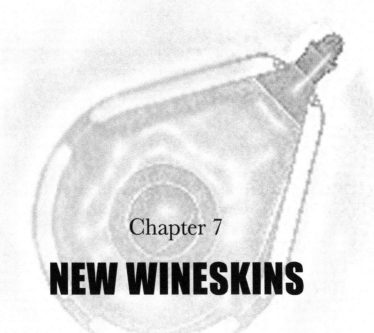

Chapter 7

NEW WINESKINS

B efore sharing this word, let's go on a quick voyage...

In April 1865, one of the most tragic maritime disasters took place. Almost 1200 people died when an explosion sank the boat they were travelling on. The Sultana was a commercial paddle-wheel steamboat that regularly carried troops during the American civil war. The boat was designed to carry 376 passengers plus crew, but was host to over 2200 people on the day it went down. Unable and ill-equipped to hold so many, the boilers exploded as it travelled on the Mississippi River, where it sank to the bottom. This is perhaps a stark reminder that vessels of any kind have constrictions and life spans. It is important to recognise when a vessel designed for a specific need, will no longer serve the purpose.

This leads me back to a word that God gave me in 2016 about what the *new* model will look like. We are not called to replicate what has gone before, although there may be reminiscence of some things, but to shift into the new.

Transforming mindsets in preparation for the new wineskin - the word God gave me in 2016

New Wineskins

I am calling you to step out of the confines of the old, and into the celebration of the new.

I am making new wineskins for new wine. The old is known, it is safe, but what is accepted is not what is best. Staying in step with Me, with My Spirit, is what I desire. See, I am doing a new thing. Do you not perceive it? There are new challenges; the new defies the recognised. The new must be discerned, for I am shifting established mindsets and reordering the thinking of My people, realigning their understanding to Mine. Do not disregard the new because it is not familiar to you. As with a new pair of shoes, they may feel tight and uncomfortable, but it is not that the fit is wrong. The new shoes may at first seem restrictive, but once you wear them you will see that it is the old that restricted you, for you have outgrown them.

The *new* is different from what you have known. My people need to ensure they do not become comfortable, for soon the old will wear out. If you do not allow me to shift you into the new, then you will miss My timing.

I am the same, yesterday, today, and forever. I do not change.

You may not quickly recognize the new because it is not what you expect. When I shift you from your comfort zone, you will know that it is I that am moving you, for My Word is constant. Look always to My Word that you might know My Ways. My Holy Spirit always moves and works in unity with My Word. For we are One. Do not be swayed by the words of men. They may sound good to the ears, but itching ears strive to hear what makes sense to the limits of man's logic and reasoning. But man's wisdom is limited. Listen, and discern what the Spirit speaks.

I am the Good Shepherd, My sheep know My voice. In this season, the harvest will be ripe. I am calling My sheep into the fold. As the sheep are drawn in, they will look for those who will teach them My ways. I am raising up shepherds after my heart; men and women that seek to lead My sheep to fresh water, so that they may drink from the well of life. You will recognize these shepherds by their hearts of compassion. They will not look to serve their own desires, but will seek to minister to the needs of others. Shepherds are not those who pursue ministry, but people. They will mingle with people without being afraid of getting their hands dirty. Their lives will reflect how Jesus walked on this earth. The Father, Jesus, and Holy Spirit; We are One. Look to My Word, and see how I walked, how I listened, how I spent My time. I did not come to this earth for ministry. My ministry was, and is, people. Many of my ministers have forgotten this truth. I came to seek and to save that which was lost; I came to rescue lives. My disciples knew Me and I knew them. The crowds flocked around Me, and I heard their cry. The bread I gave them was not about feeding five thousand hungry stomachs, but hungry hearts. I saw their plight and My heart filled with compassion, so I fed them the Word. I saw their need and healed the sick. I taught the people and showed them how to live, by example.

So many of My ministers think that standing in a pulpit is what leadership is about, but they have forgotten the model that I taught them. Despite being surrounded by crowds, I saw the individual. I took time to listen. Many of my ministers have not learned how to listen. Shepherds listen out for the flock; they recognize the bleats and understand the need. So too, my shepherds listen to the sheep in the flock under their care, for they look out for the sheep. When you truly listen, you will know how to respond. You will know the word in season. When you speak, let people know that you hear. When I spoke to the woman at the well, I did not judge or condemn her, I let her hear that I knew her. This is what transforms. It is in the knowing. In knowing others, you will know Me. This is the key into the hearts of man. (man= humankind).

Many of my ministers do not know their flock. They are quick to judge what they do not know, what they do not understand. But those I am positioning will know the sheep under their care. Allow My Holy

Spirit to flood you with My love. You cannot love in your own strength. Let My unconditional love move you, as a mother who does not condemn the child she once nursed at her breast, even though they stray. So you, too, nurture your flock and allow Me to give you a mother's heart. The father of the prodigal son saw him when he was still a great way off, and had compassion. This story reflects the Father heart of God, My heart. Allow Me to give you My Father's heart. Do not be afraid, for I have chosen you. I have called you by name.

I am shaping My Church; preparing My bride for My return. The current model does not yet fully reflect My glory. Too many have created a hierarchical system based on worldly ideals. Leaders have raised themselves into positions, labelling themselves with titles that I have not given them. It is by their fruit that you will know them. Therefore, be wise who you join yourself to. Many I have chosen and am calling in this day are those who have been passed by. I am raising those who have been trained in the desert and the wilderness. I am calling those who are weak, those who seem foolish, to shame the wise. For it is not man's strength or wisdom that will stand in the latter days. It is only those who know their weakness and walk according to My Spirit, which is their strength. So, in your weakness lean on Me, as we journey together. Let Me lead you into uncharted waters that will cause you to rise to new heights in My Spirit. As you rise, you will lead others into new depths. In the new wineskin, I will pour new wine and...

"I pray that you, being rooted and established in love, may have power, together with all the Lord's holy people, to grasp how wide and long and high and deep is the love of Christ, and to know this love that surpasses knowledge—that you may be filled to the measure of all the fullness of God."
Ephesians 3: 18-19 (NIV)

JOURNAL YOUR THOUGHTS

BIBLE

PRAYER

8 ~

Chapter 8

BIRTHING

Let's circle back for a moment to the Sultana. This boat should have been retired or at least used for the limited number of passengers it was intended for, and multiple lives wouldn't have been lost. Do you know what happens to boats that are no longer seaworthy? They usually end up in the boat graveyard, where they are used for parts. However, some have been given a new lease of life, being transformed and given fresh purpose.

In 2016 I recorded an artist performing on board the 1950's German cargo ship moored in Bristol's harbour. *The Thekla* has been lovingly given a new lease of life as a music venue and nightclub. Similar to the Thekla, many other boats have been restored with new significance. Although many have been sunk, even creating artificial barrier reefs, there are cruise liners that have been recycled into floating hotels. Others have been used during disasters, in relief efforts such as those after a hurricane, or used as hospitals. What wonderful ways to resurrect these boats after the end of an era of shipping passengers, to then be of service in new ways. Yet note each one had to undergo a renewal. The old wineskin wasn't fit for its original purpose and needed to be made new for its next mission.

As God reminded me about the **new wineskins** He'd spoken to me about back then, I began to see that God was downloading **blueprints** to many people. These were new ministries, often designed in the form of businesses to be an impartation of the divine on earth. I could see these blueprinted businesses providing much needed creative solutions to many needs. **These were to become arks that would bring hope and life to others.** Some were specifically aimed at equipping and supporting the body of Christ, whilst others were being prepared to meet the needs of the world. This was across multiple industries and sectors of society. I could see holy blueprint solutions helping to create a rich tapestry that reflects the love God has for His creation.

The world began to see the Father, as the Church began to rise in the love ministry of offering much needed solutions to the overwhelming problems that are prevalent in our societies. All around I started to see spiritual pregnancies. Both men and women were carrying these in their spirits. It is something much greater than natural child bearing - each was carrying spiritual babies and some carried them together in pairs or small numbers. These spiritual babies would give birth to eternal fruit and a harvest of life.

Jesus used parables to explain the everyday in a way that made sense to those He spoke to. This image is one that you can glean from, since we understand the pattern of natural childbirth, it helps us to better comprehend what is happening in the Spirit realm. Do you sense something being birthed in your life?

We read in *Isaiah 66* about how the Nation of Israel is prophesied about by using the same birthing analogy.

> *"Before she goes into labour, she gives birth.*
> *Before the pains come upon her, she delivers*
> *a son. Who has ever heard such things?*
> *Who has ever seen things like this? Can a*
> *country be born in a day? or a nation be*
> *brought forth in a moment? Yet no sooner*
> *is Zion in labour then she gives birth to*
> *her children. Do I bring to the moment of*
> *birth, and not give delivery?" says the Lord.*
> *"Do I close up the womb when I bring to*
> *delivery?" says your God.*
> *Isaiah 66:7-9 (NIV)*

This scripture reminds us that God will not bring to the point of birth and not deliver. So, you can be encouraged that He will bring forth that which He has spoken. But we are also reminded through this scripture that there are birthing pains. So, again this can help you to discern when you go through all kinds of trials and travail that these are often representative of the **birthing pains** you need to go through, in order to bring forth the new life.

Anyone who has established a business or ministry already will understand the challenges and hurdles that can cause new ventures to abort. We need to be mindful that we are in a spiritual battle and the enemy would seek to cause spiritual abortions, but we don't walk in fear, but in faith for He who began this good work, will continue it in us - and the things God is causing us to birth, He will bring through to delivery. It is therefore essential that you recognise what will help us bring forth healthy babies.

It's a good reminder that what you may be carrying must be born by the Spirit and not by your own desires or will.

> *"So he said to me, 'This is the Word of the Lord to Zerubbabel saying, 'Not by might nor by power, but by My Spirit,' says the Lord Almighty"*
> *Zechariah 4:6 (NIV)*

As with any pregnancy, the mother needs to look after herself, in order to nourish and protect the precious baby within. We too should keep the dreams from God protected and hidden until the point of delivery. Trying to deliver too soon when the baby is not full term, will risk their life. We also need to feed both ourselves, and the baby: ensuring we are in right relationship with God, and with others; feeding on the Word; being nourished in praise and worship; keeping connected with our spiritual leaders and peers, *Hebrews 10: 25*; and additionally, taking rest.

Rest is essential to a healthy birth. When I was pregnant there were points when I slept more hours a day than I was awake. Being still, and letting God do the work in breathing life and growing the *baby* within, keeps us at His feet.

Why is this so important?

God revealed to me how many know they are being called into a new pace and space of rest, but to understand more clearly, is to see this birthing analogy. When we rest, we are giving the reins to God. We cannot control the minute when a baby will be brought forth from the womb. God alone knows when a child is conceived and when they will enter the world. Every day of their life is already written by God, *Psalm 139:16*.

When you **take time to rest and live out of a place of rest**, you are saying, I am not going to strive to complete this (whatever it may be), in my way or on my time scale. It causes you to **let go of control** and ultimately, you are aligned more fully with the Almighty. It is to Him alone that all the glory must go.

Pride is subtle and can creep up on us when we least expect it. So not taking time to rest when our brain tells us we *should* be working, can be a sign of pride. I am not talking about laziness or procrastination, that is another issue I'm not going to address now. We have spent so long being driven (by self) that we are having to readjust to the new dispensation - the spiritual reordering of natural things - and that includes time! **God is re-ordering our time.**

My prayer is that you are encouraged by seeing the bigger picture of what God is doing in our time. This moment in which we are alive on this earth. It is exciting. There are numerous dreams that are being, and about to be, birthed. Many of you have held on to these for many years and have been weary in believing, thinking perhaps you had got it wrong, or missed the opportunity.

In *Genesis 18:12* you can read about how Sarah laughed when the Lord and two angels appeared and she heard that she would bear a son, since she was past the age of childbearing. But then in *Hebrews* see how it attests to her trust in the faithfulness of God.

"And by faith even Sarah, who was past

childbearing age, was enabled to bear
children because she considered him faithful
who had made the promise".
Hebrews 11:11 (NIV)

God will often allow impossible situations to provide opportunities for the miraculous. He alone deserves the glory.

JOURNAL YOUR THOUGHTS

BIBLE

PRAYER

9 ~

Chapter 9

THE ORPHAN SPIRIT

After receiving the words following my little adventure to see the ark, I leaned into the Spirit to download the blueprint.

A little side note here that may help you recognise when God is doing this in your life. You may remember when we could first connect to the Web via the Internet; it was painfully slow. When you opened an email that contained an attachment there was no instant access. You had to wait for the attachment to download. That process could be painstaking. I remember spending hours upon hours staring at a strip of empty bars on my screen, each one representing how far the download was to completion. You never knew if it was an image or piece of text that would appear. Only once the download finished could it be opened. Then what had been sent would be revealed. It was impossible to use the computer for anything else whilst the download was taking place.

For me, the process of receiving a download from God is very much like this. Until it's completely finished downloading, I am unable to do much else. There's a sense of waiting, knowing that He is downloading something into my spirit. Once the process is complete, it's as if the Holy Spirit then opens it up before me, so that I can see and hear clearly what the message contains. When we recognise that there is a download happening, there can be a sense of weightiness. Something is being received into our spirits ready to be birthed.

There is more to be taken from this analogy. Originally, when home computers began connecting to their LAN (Local Area Network) the cable went via the landline. This was the main connection for home phones, which meant you couldn't connect your computer to the Internet and be on your telephone at the same time. There were no ethernet splitters or Wi-Fi, so if you were working online or surfing the Web and the phone rang, you'd be kicked off and could potentially lose all of your work. For me, I remember watching those download bars go up to 90% only to go back to 0% when the phone rang. Talk about frustration, eh?

But this serves to explain my next point. If God is downloading something into your spirit, wanting to **communicate to you**, and you attempt to focus on other distractions, you can lose the momentum and potentially only receive a proportion of what the Holy Spirit intended to impart. **Discerning when the Lord is speaking** and discerning the appropriate action (even rest) is essential to receiving the fullness of what God intends for you.

Whilst receiving the blueprint download God was speaking to me about, I could feel the spiritual birthing pains in my life. However, I became aware that there was a blockage and a friend told me they could see something was holding me back. I sat on the little sofa in my office and asked the Lord, "what is this obstacle that seems to be blocking the way?"

Immediately, I heard an inner voice say, "orphan spirit" and instantaneously I broke down and wept. However, I was confused because I'd received healing over 30 years ago from when my earthly father abandoned me. Quickly, the Holy Spirit unpacked where it had come from. The tears fell as I received deep healing from what He showed me.

For many years I have carried a vision deep inside of me. It was ignited during my early years as a believer when I was released into full-time ministry [aside: I believe we are all in full-time ministry if our lives are submitted to doing God's will, no matter what job that entails]. I experienced amazing doors of favour open and I was able to share the word of God to millions, before royalty, when I was just twenty years old. However, although I've experienced seasons of favour, I've also had to walk through many painful Joseph years. I may not have been sold into slavery or put in prison, but I have had to walk a specifically challenging journey that caused me to feel ostracised by those around me. Those I expected to be there to help me in my time of need were often those I felt judged by. The loneliness of being misunderstood on many levels, with my calling hidden from others, meant I felt rejected. I knew there were things God called me to carry alone, but I didn't realise the burden of it had brought about this orphan mentality.

I sat on the little sofa in my office, allowing wave after wave of healing permeate my soul, as God revealed to me how He was connecting me into the body of Christ around the world.

Have you ever felt like Elijah when he ran and hid in the cave thinking he was the only prophet left?

> *"I have been very zealous for the Lord God*
> *Almighty. The Israelites have rejected your*
> *covenant, torn down your altars, and put*
> *your prophets to death with the sword. I am*
> *the only one left, and now they are trying to*
> *kill me too."*
> *1 Kings 19:14 (NIV)*

I certainly wasn't thinking of myself as a prophet, though I know that God speaks to me prophetically. But I did feel isolated and alone. Once I'd received my healing, I discovered a new found joy and God showed me, like Elijah, that there were many others feeling the same as I had been, struggling with isolation, as the enemy had sought to cause separation. Please note here, I am not pointing a finger to anyone who may have judged me or rejected me. Often our perceptions are not fact - but it is to recognise how the enemy has been actively attacking God's people. He revealed to me that the **orphan spirit** is something that is rampant and not something that was peculiar to me. It is a spirit sent to thwart mindsets, causing people to feel cast off and alone. I share this to help you **discern** what the enemy has been seeking to do, to **separate and isolate; to cause rejection and self-pity.**

> *"Yet I reserve seven thousand in Israel—all*
> *whose knees have not bowed down to Baal*
> *and whose mouths have not kissed him."*
> *1 Kings 18 (NIV)*

Elijah felt alone, but in reality, there were another seven thousand just like him!

Even Paul recognises that separation can cause us to feel like orphans.

> *"But, brothers and sisters, when we were*
> *orphaned by being separated from you for a*
> *short time (in person, not in thought), out*
> *of our intense longing we made every effort*
> *to see you."*
> *1 Thessalonians 2:17 (NIV)*

The good news is that God is connecting the Church like never before. The barriers are being removed. The online space can connect us in ways we could not have perceived before the millennium in 2000. The warning though is this...

Do not judge.

Do not judge what you do not understand and what you do not know fully. Do not judge one another, only God alone is the One who sits on the judgement seat. I encourage you to acknowledge it, if you've held judgement in your heart, or you identify with feeling orphaned in any way. I know many of you will feel the deep sense of anguish and pain I felt, but this is a time for healing. It is essential to repent of any judgement, let go of self-pity and forgive those who've wounded you. God can fully heal and restore you, as you come honestly and openly to Him. Release all that you carry. The Lord wants you to be whole, to be free and fully prepared, because the promised land is in sight.

Why is this so important?

On my office whiteboard there is a little piece of paper with the definition of the word orphan on it. This is what it says:

orphan
noun \ ´ȯr-fən \
one deprived of protection or advantage

Years ago, I filmed in Sri Lanka and set up a charity to help those who'd become orphans as a result of the 2004 tsunami. But since then, I realised there is an entire generation of orphans in our own neighbourhoods. Not just those who are parentless, but those who are orphaned in spirit. The definition on the note attached to my board says: **one deprived of protection or advantage.** Having worked with children and young people over many years, engaging with social services and as a teacher, I am acutely aware of the amount of deprivation and lack of protection we have on our own doorsteps.

Even in our own families and churches, there are those who are starving through lack. Not only starved of food, but of love, care, affection, and all manner of parenting. Sadly, many also lack the protection that should be every child's right. This is why it is so important that we are nourished by the Holy Spirit who is our counsellor and friend, and in our relationships with one another. There is an orphaned generation who needs us.

Notwithstanding the rising numbers of abuse and neglect, I've seen too many role reversals with children having to shoulder the responsibility for their parents. High numbers of young people are worrying about money and other adult issues. Whether they are their parents' carer or living with a single parent who has to work; coming back from school to empty homes; or making their own meals and struggling to keep up with their studies, they are learning about life from the Internet instead of from family. They carry burdens that aren't theirs, instead of playing and having fun. The lack of nurturing in our communities is at an all-time low. This impacts negatively on a child's development, resulting in psychological and behavioural issues that, in turn, damage society.

Years ago, there was a greater sense of community following two world wars. I remember my grandma telling me stories about how, after the war, people pulled together to help one another. This time of great loss and devastation drew them closer, as a community. Instead of drawing each to their own homes, they looked outwardly, offering support for those around them. What she described reminds me of the quote, "It takes a village to raise a child." Surely, this is a scriptural image of the family of God coming together, to love the world in which we've been placed.

It is time to say, orphans no more. It is time to let those who are orphaned know that there is a worldwide family waiting to embrace them. Let's first embrace one another.

Kick out any mindset that says you are alone. You may feel rejected, but if you've accepted Jesus as your Saviour, there is a worldwide family of Christ that you belong to. You are not alone.

JOURNAL YOUR THOUGHTS

BIBLE

PRAYER

10 ~

Chapter 10

A NEW PERSPECTIVE

Some years ago, I opened my curtains and looked out into the Spring sky from my bedroom window. The sky was a pretty blue with several white clouds drifting slowly across it. As I gazed, a glint of light radiating from the sun caught my eye. It pierced through the clouds and lit up parts of the sky. Suddenly, I saw something else in the vast expanse before me. I felt translated into a moment, where I could see a massive army dressed in shining battle armour; an angelic host. I could feel the sense of anticipation coming from the multitude of angels. They were holding shields in their hands with swords at the ready. Light illuminated around them. They were prepared; they were ready for battle. There was an air of excitement because they knew they were about to be released for battle, and the angels knew they had already won. Not only did they outnumber the enemy forces, but they had seen the end.

Victory was assured.

Although the time had not yet come *(at that time)* for them to wage this battle, I knew it was soon. They were expectant, waiting for their commanding officer to signal the trumpet sound, to advance. Immediately following this insight, I heard a frightful sound. It was like a squealing pig. I knew it was demonic. It resounded across the atmosphere and I could see a swirling in the invisible realm, as the embodiment of the sound raced around in panic. In an instant I knew what it was. The enemy could see the huge army of the Lord, strong and ready for battle. Its fate had been sealed and its time running out. In a last-ditch effort, I could see that it was seeking to intimidate and disempower anyone in its wake. Those who the enemy was attacking couldn't necessarily see that it was a defeated foe coming against them. They didn't realise that an angelic force was moving in to fight on their behalf. The squealing demonic hoard was implementing every conniving scheme and tactic it could muster. It was haphazardly lashing out with every weapon it had at its disposal, in its final showdown.

I remembered watching a world war film when I was young. The only thing I can remember was the final scene when war had been clearly won, but the fighting continued. The guards in the concentration camps didn't let on to their captives that the liberating army was on its way. They continued to torment the prisoners, treating them like slaves as they vented their hatred and bitterness towards them. If you only see the enemy's attack, you can be overcome, paralysed with fear. When you look up and hear the sound of victory, you are strengthened in the resolve to stand firm, awaiting your deliverance from the tyranny.

God will often allow impossible situations to provide opportunities for the miraculous. Miracles are the result of a need for divine intervention. He alone deserves the glory.

The sense of moving towards a promised land is strong and many voices are now echoing what I have seen in the Spirit for a number of years. Yet it is important to discern what this looks like. After all, we can hear about a land flowing with milk and honey, a time of rest and restoration, abundance, revival or whatever, and get fired up. But if you don't discern what that looks like in reality, and see the bigger picture, you may struggle to enter in and reap the fruit.

So what will the promised land look like? How will you recognise it? What should you expect when you arrive?

The hope of a promised land is all very well, but you need to discern so much more about what that means. The reality is that many people feel as if there is a fog before them, they are unable to see clearly. Some are pushing through the fog and others are feeling stagnant and discouraged, not knowing what to do. Still others are excitedly moving forward, with the hope of a promised land. But it's important to see the bigger picture. As a filmmaker, I understand the importance of being able to zoom out to allow the audience to see the wider view. From a director's perspective, I need to be fully aware of what is also going on *off-camera*. What is happening out of sight is just as important as what is going on in plain view. Both are essential to the story.

We can glean from the parallel of the story through Exodus when the children of Israel, led by Moses, journeyed to the promised land. It's interesting to note as we read through Exodus, when the Israelites left Egypt in pursuit of the promised land that God led them with a pillar of cloud. I don't know if you like to peer out of the window on a flight and watch as the plane soars above the clouds, but

I do. When the plane pushes through those clouds, before it emerges above the blanket in the sky, there's a moment of fog, through which it is impossible to see clearly. Without its navigational system the plane would be flying blind. It's like trying to peer through a thick haze, until suddenly you have to shield your eyes from the intense light of the sun, as the plane pierces through the clouds. The sun was always there, even when I couldn't see it through the cloud.

God is leading us again with his pillar of cloud. Do not expect to see clearly until you have risen above. But listen for His voice:

> *"Whether you turn to the right or to the*
> *left, your ears will hear a voice behind you,*
> *saying, "This is the way; walk in it."*
> *Isaiah 30:21 (NIV)*

In 2016, I began to hear **a new sound**. I could hear the sound of a shofar in the spirit. The shofar is an instrument made from a ram's horn. Many bibles translate it as a trumpet. The shofar has different blasts that are used to signify different things. At the time, I didn't really know anything about the shofar, but the sound was resonating in my spirit. I sensed it was **a call to awaken.** *THIS* is the sound I've been mentioning throughout this book that I told you earlier I'd explain.

Interestingly, that same year I attended a small home church study group. I'd never attended the group before and never got to attend again, since it wasn't a local one. Despite only being a handful of us in attendance, I carried great expectancy in my spirit. As I closed my eyes in worship, I could hear the sound of the shofar in my spirit. Almost immediately, whilst being led to release a prophetic word about the shofar call, I heard a stronger sound of the shofar behind me. I was confused and couldn't tell if it was real or in my mind. After sharing the word that was impressed upon my spirit, I eventually opened my eyes, but couldn't see where the sound had been coming from, despite us being huddled together in a small living room. It was only later I discovered that someone had indeed brought a shofar and played it during the meeting.

During that time, the Lord impressed on my spirit that there would be a new sound calling out to His people. **A call to return to your first love and a summoning.** The Lord impressed on my spirit that there would also be **a new sound ushering in a new era**. We will reap if we walk in step with the new rhythm. Can you hear the call of the trumpet, the shofar, and the beat of the drum? It's time to join together to shift into the Promised Land, walk in your anointing, and fulfil the call of service to see the harvest fields reaped for eternal purpose.

It's time to gain **a new perspective**.

What I sensed of the new did not look the same, it did not sound the same, it did not smell the same. In fact, what I saw was so different that it was almost unrecognisable. Familiarity was gone. We need to understand that where we are headed, where we are transitioning to is not where we have come from. If we do not discern the time that we are in and what God is doing, we may not **recognise the destination**.

In the spring of 2005, I stood alone on a vast beach looking out to the Laccadive Sea (in the northern part of the Indian Ocean). It was glorious. There was a breeze, but the sun shone bright in the sky. It was hot with miles of golden sunlit sand stretched out before me. I set up my camera and tripod to film, with not another soul in sight. I was all alone on this beautiful shore in what should have been the beginning of the tourist season. All I could hear was the sound of the waves crashing onto the beach. "Today, I stand here alone..." I began my piece to camera. Alone, because everyone else, even my driver and interpreter, were too afraid to join me. I was standing on a beautiful beach that didn't even exist four months earlier. But its beauty was unseen because it signified terror. In as much as this beach had appeared over a period of 24 hours, other local beaches had disappeared. They no longer existed. They had been engulfed by the ravaging sea in the 2004 Boxing Day Tsunami taking with them approx 35,000 lives in Sri Lanka alone. Almost 230,000 lives were tragically lost that day, throughout the countries impacted by the Indian Ocean earthquake and tsunamis that ensued. The horror of what I saw on that trip is a stark reminder that nobody knows what can happen **in an instant**. But we can be prepared for what lies ahead because we have the Spirit of God.

I was in awe of the Churches there, who gave no thought of their own comfort, to step up and **be the difference** in their county. I watched horrific video footage of them literally pulling truckloads of dead bodies out of the waterways, and listened to heartbreaking stories. The sight was beyond imagination. I was grateful I didn't have to smell what they described. But members of the congregation didn't hesitate. They rolled up their sleeves and did whatever was necessary. They also set up camps for hundreds of people who'd lost family and homes. I stayed the night in one of the camps and toured around the island, listening to heart wrenching stories of loss. Even the very clothes on their body had been swept off those who'd miraculously survived being submerged in the torrent. Others, like a young lad

I interviewed, had clung to the top of a tall palm tree that saved his life. Sadly, many of the children that survived were now orphans.

For the Christian community, a deep sense of what is truly important, stuck out. They demonstrated love for their brothers and sisters, of any religion or belief, despite their faith being on the receiving end of hate crimes prior to this. They embraced humanity with the love of God; they helped people find hope again. They sought to build an orphanage, re-build houses, create business opportunities, provide care and much more. What I witnessed was a Christ centred community who spoke at least three different languages (holding different services for each), creating an Ark of rescue. Their outlook and perspective of life had changed for all. The landscape was no longer the same as it had been at the end of 2004. Priorities were being re-aligned to what is truly important, to what holds **eternal value**.

Just like those beaches in Sri Lanka, our landscape is about to change. If you look out to sea from the beach, your perspective will change if you then look at the same view from the cliffs above. Same view, different perspective. The future holds a new environment to what we've previously known. God wants to take you higher to see more from His perspective.

Are you ready to see through new eyes and to look from a new perspective?

And when we rise "...the light of the sun will be seven times brighter."

Isaiah 30:26 (AMP)

JOURNAL YOUR THOUGHTS

BIBLE

PRAYER

11 ~

Chapter 11

THE PROMISED LAND

Iremember leaving home for the first time. The excitement of independence, having my own apartment, within which I created my own little sanctuary. I was able to manage my own mealtimes and bedtime without it impacting on anyone else. I was free!

Well, yes it was exciting and yes it was a fantastic time in my life. I joined a full-time ministry touring the country, performing and sharing my faith. But moving home perhaps wasn't quite as fun and carefree. There were the practical aspects that I had to deal with, such as all the legalities of changing address. I had to manage my finances and pay bills that I'd never had before. Everyone in the ministry lived by faith, so I had to step up to a new level of trusting God for all my needs. My budget was practically non-existent, so the disposable income I'd previously lavished on myself wasn't there. Trusting God for my daily bread was literally where I was at. I remember walking around the local minimarket scouring the aisles for any bargains I could find. Over the years, I've learnt how to spot them well, ha-ha. Budgeting and buying my own food, clothes, bills, and running my car (which at the time was both an essential and miracle provision), were all fresh experiences for me.

These responsibilities were not the only new things that stretched me. Touring was an adventure. I loved it, but it is not the glamorous lifestyle many envision. In reality, I came home, usually in the early hours, to a cold and empty apartment. I'd have to park my car up the hill and walk down a couple of winding back-alleys leading to my small, two-storey annexed apartment in the dark. There was no warm welcome on my return. No music from the radio waking me up with my mother making breakfast in the morning. No sounds of my sisters laughing, arguing, or watching TV.

Just silence.

Not just the sounds, but the entire location was **unfamiliar.** I'd been brought up in southeast London, in a built-up area full of people and activity. Now, I was in the little town of Malmesbury in Wiltshire, surrounded by old stone buildings and countryside. It was strange and different. Instead of police sirens and traffic, I heard the birds singing. Even the people spoke differently, and I don't just mean their accent.

On my way to the village shops, I'd regularly hear "Mornin'", or "Af'ernoon", as I passed the locals. Despite being surrounded by people where I'd grown up, it was unusual to hear strangers speak to me. This was something I grew to love about the place, being part of a small community, where everyone says hello and gives a friendly smile.

The air even smelt different, as the countryside aromas (or rather animal odours) filled the air.

The transition was an interesting time. It took me a while to acclimatise to all the changes. Before moving, there was much I could never have conceived in advance. Yet, it was a rich time of blessing and many of the new changes I enjoyed. More than anything I was privileged to experience a powerful move of God through the ministry He led us in. Numerous (in their hundreds) predominantly young people would run to the altar (front of the stage). Tears streamed as they cried out to God to be saved. Instantaneous prophetic utterances from the mouths of those who'd just surrendered their lives, was common. There were times when the Holy Spirit supernaturally took over, disrupting our plans and taking things in God's pre-ordained direction. The result was healings and miracles, as captives were set free, and lives were transformed.

As we now look to the promised land, in this time, there is a parallel to discern. When you shift from one place to another, there will be changes that you can't foresee. Being prepared to move requires you to be equipped and ready for what awaits you. There will be rich blessings, but it will not be everything you imagine. It will be better, but not necessarily what you expect. There will also be giants.

This is a time of transition

There are those who remember Egypt. You could perhaps say it (Egypt) represents a time before the Web. You could perhaps say that it was a period where *time* itself was the perpetual slave master. The reality is that each of our Egypt's are different, it does not look the same as another's. There are still those who have wandered through the wilderness that don't remember a time back in Egypt. Yet each of the different generations will journey together into all that God has spoken. You may recognise the Moses' era is coming to completion, as the Joshua and Caleb era is breaking forth. Many of our generals have been taken home; promoted to glory. We are now challenged to take up the baton and overcome with faith, not shrink from fear.

This is the transition; the space between, before you cross over. This will be both individual and corporate. The same and yet different. Just as lockdown was the same for everyone, yet dissimilar in experience. For some, it was a dream come true, whilst for others it was a nightmare experience. Being prepared, forewarned, and equipped will enable you to be planted in the land, **positioned for purpose**.

Before entering into the land God had promised to the Israelites, Moses sent out a party to inspect the territory. He gave them a set of instructions to check out various aspects of both the land and the people who lived there. The leaders from each of the tribes went for forty days to investigate, returning with a report on what they found.

> *"We went to the land where you sent us.*
> *It really is a land flowing with milk and*
> *honey. Here's some of its fruit."*
> *Numbers 13:27 (NIV).*

However, as you probably are aware it wasn't the good report you'd expect from the place God had promised them. The majority of the search party returned with a very large BUT...

...filled with excuses and fear!

"**But** the people who live there are strong, and the cities have walls and are very large. We even saw the descendants of Anak there. The Amalekites live in the Negev. The Hittites, Jebusites, and Amorites live in the mountain region. And the Canaanites live along the coast of the Mediterranean Sea and all along the Jordan River."
Numbers 13:28-29 (NIV)

However, Caleb arose and said,

> *"'Let's go now and take possession of the land. We should be more than able to conquer it.' BUT the men who had gone with him said, 'We can't attack those people! They're too strong for us!'"*
> *Numbers 13: 30-31 (NIV)*

We clearly see here a statement of faith rebuffed with another BUT!

Regardless of the two young men of faith, Caleb and Joshua, pleading God's cause, the rest of the men remained adamant in their unbelief. Fear had taken hold of them. **They believed their own eyes rather than the eyes of faith.** They trusted in their lack of ability to conquer the land, as opposed to depending on the One who had made a covenant with them. Does that resonate with you? Do you trust in your circumstances or do you put your faith in the one who is faithful, despite what the natural situation may scream in your face? We are living in the days when you need to discern what you see with your physical eyes, with spiritual eyes. And what you hear with your physical ears, you should discern with your spiritual ears.

*"Obey what I command you today. I
will drive out before you the Amorites,
Canaanites, Hittites, Perizzites, Hivites
and Jebusites. Be careful not to make a
treaty with those who live in the land where
you are going, or they will be a snare among
you."*
Exodus 34:12 (NIV)

These are the words that God spoke when the children of
Israel entered the promised land. He warned them to drive
out the giants, or else they would be a snare (a trap) to them.

What can we learn from this?

We are about to, and are, entering, the **promised land**,
the place beyond our Egypt and wilderness. It will not be
recognisable by what we already know or understand.
Within that space of unfamiliarity there will be giants.
These won't necessarily be large armies of people, but
giants of fear, confusion, intimidation, temptation, idolatry,
pride, defilement, carnality, apathy and more.

You can learn from history. The Israelites spent years
wandering in the wilderness, because although they were
dressed for battle, their hearts were weak and they would
have fled at the sight of war *Exodus 13:17*. So God led them
via the desert and the Red Sea. Yes, God was angry with
their lack of faith, but I see here a demonstration of His
love and grace. He knew that they'd have been overcome
had they attempted to enter the promised land **before**
they were ready. Graciously, He trained them in the desert.
He taught them about His faithfulness, so that the next
generation were equipped to enter their inheritance.

This is why you have walked your journey. He has trained you for battle. **God has been teaching you to trust Him**. You are being taught by the Lord in the school of life. Before David ever encountered Goliath, he'd been trained to overcome the lion and the bear, whilst in obscurity caring for the sheep. When he faced his biggest giant, guess what? He wasn't afraid! He had learnt to have faith in God because he had learnt how to overcome. See how David responds to King Saul, who tells him,

> *"You are not able to go out against this*
> *Philistine and fight him; you are only a*
> *young man, and he has been a warrior from*
> *his youth."*
> *1 Samuel 17: 33 (NIV)*

> *"Your servant has been keeping his father's*
> *sheep. When a lion or a bear came and*
> *carried off a sheep from the flock, I went*
> *after it, struck it and rescued the sheep from*
> *its mouth. When it turned on me, I seized*
> *it by its hair, struck it and killed it. **Your***
> ***servant has killed both the lion***
> ***and the bear; this uncircumcised***
> ***Philistine will be like one of them**,*
> *because he has defied the armies of the*
> *living God. The Lord who rescued me from*
> *the paw of the lion and the paw of the*
> *bear will rescue me from the hand of this*
> *Philistine."*
> *1 Samuel 17: 34-37 (NIV)*

There are so many examples through the Bible of how God trained His people for purpose. Joseph wasn't a wise steward or powerful leader when his brothers tried to kill him. He learnt how to overcome adversity, to forgive what seemed unforgivable, and how to steward honourably **in the secret place**, being put in charge of the other prisoners. Just have a good read of *Genesis 39-41*.

Wow, what a journey of preparation, to be positioned in Pharaoh's palace as his right-hand man. Why? So that Joseph could be God's instrument to save His children, the Israelites, so they didn't perish in the famine that the Lord knew was coming.

So, guess what?

There are things on the way that *only* God knows. Who knew that in 2020 the world would face a global scale virus and lockdowns? **It is time to discern and be prepared for what lies ahead.**

Beloved, it is time for the Spirit-led leaders to arise. We have shifted, and are shifting, into a new dispensation; a divine re-ordering of natural things. God has been re-ordering your life and removing the slave mentality of Egypt. Let me tell you a secret... **you weren't ready before!**

Like the children of Israel, you'd have fainted in the battle.

> *"God did not lead them on the road through the Philistine country, though that was shorter. For God said, 'If they face war, they might change their minds and return to Egypt.'"*
> *Exodus 13:17 (NIV)*

Now the promised land is in sight, but there are defeated giants to overthrow. Through the hard place, you have been honed. You have come through the fire to be brought forth like gold. God is raising up an army of warriors. He is raising up the prophetic, the creatives, leaders, and entrepreneurs; those who will pioneer something new that will communicate God's heart. This will be through leaders that know how to walk in their anointing, humility, and grace.

If this resonates with you then, it's time to ensure that you are equipped and prepared to shift into your destiny. You know you're carrying a promise that is too big for you to birth alone. It's as if you've been pregnant for years and now you can feel the labour pains. But we were never meant to do this alone. You may have carried this baby alone in the wilderness, but we all need spiritual midwives to help us when it comes to our time of delivery. We need one another.

JOURNAL YOUR THOUGHTS

BIBLE

PRAYER

12 ~

Chapter 12

TESTUDO

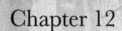

The image God gave me in 2015 when He first arrested my attention and began to unfold all that I am laying out before you in this book, was that of the Roman **Testudo**. The Roman soldiers would create a hedge of protection around themselves and each other, with their shields. They would move towards the enemy in this tortoise style formation, which was practically impenetrable to the arrows from their foe. If we walk arm in arm, linked shield to shield protecting each other, then we can advance into the land with confidence.

Remaining isolated makes you vulnerable to attack. Compromise is less likely if you have accountability. The children of Israel compromised their faith, by allowing foreign gods to become a snare. They began to serve Baals and Asherahs, forgetting the Lord their God, *Judges 3*.

Deborah was a great woman of faith. She was a prophetess and judge, *Judges 4-5*. When the heart of Barak, the leader of the military army failed, Deborah rose to the call. She accompanied the army into battle, and their enemy was defeated. God is raising up men and women, young and old, in this time. Those who have been trained in the desert and the wilderness; those who have grown in faith, knowing the faithfulness of their Saviour. Barak's faith was weaker and he needed another leader to stand with him. This is a time when it is important to find others to stand with and alongside you, because together we are stronger. Together, our faith is multiplied. The enemy has been on a mission to divide, to separate, but this is a time of seeing what joins us. Seek the commonality, not the difference.

As the saying goes, "united we stand, divided we fall." This isn't a direct quote from the Bible, but the truth it carries certainly is.

The story of the tower of Babel in *Genesis 11* clearly presents the power of unity and working together for one purpose. Famously in *verse 5*, God lets us know that nothing is impossible for those who come together in one accord. If that is the consequence of heathens working together, can you imagine the power of faith-filled believers joining in unity for **one purpose** under Heaven in the name of Jesus. What impact could be made for good, if united together we demonstrated God's love and served our fellow man? Then why do we allow so much to bring division? Why do we hold so tight to our self-opinionated thinking and beliefs? Do you expect others to take the first step, or how is the Holy Spirit speaking to you?

Matthew 12:25 and *Luke 11:17* clearly lay out that a kingdom divided against itself won't stand. It is vital that we each harness our own responsibility to recognise if we are allowing any grievances, mindsets, or behaviours that are hindering God's heart for unity. Discernment is needed to understand what that looks like for *you*, because none of us can judge another's response. We each stand, alone before the Father, as He searches the **intention of the heart**.

The ultimate reason for this chapter is to **discern the strategy,** the blueprint for successfully entering into the promised land. In *Joshua 9* you will find the key to opening the door to all that the Lord has for you. Remember the Israelites were told to conquer the enemy so that they wouldn't be entangled by their snares. Verse 14 tells us why they failed. They didn't enquire of the Lord. If you enquire of God before you take action, you're honouring the One who is the commander in chief. You're putting Him in the driving seat of your life.

The Israelites were deceived by their enemy who lied to them saying they lived far away, when indeed they dwelt nearby, but God already knew that. And **He alone knows what you don't. He sees what you can't.** The loving Father wants to protect you.

Reading through the *Book of Joshua*, you can see how the Israelite army worked through the land, bit by bit, claiming the territory that was already theirs. The enemy you face is not a physical one. You are not fighting flesh and blood, but there is a spiritual battle warring around you. For example, the mental health issues prevalent in society is a direct attack on our communities. Fear, anxiety, and self-harm are all enemies.

These enemies need armies to defeat them; armies of believers joined together with their shields linked in a testudo formation. In any army there are commanders, generals, lieutenants, sergeants, infantry and so forth. Each one has their position. Whether they are a combat soldier on foot, cavalry on horseback, or an officer motivating and making strategic decisions, each has an important part to play. Every individual needs to be in their position so that the army can successfully function. A shoddy army is most likely a defeated one. A defeated army is at the mercy of the victor.

Why is it so important that we join together as we shift into the 'new'?

The enemy is sneaky and uses subtle (as well as blatant) temptations. In addition to the mental health issues, there is a growing level of addictions and compulsive behaviours that are prevalent in our society. These bring with them a weight of shame that seeks to isolate. There are also hidden temptations, such as the state of the heart. Envy may not be obvious, but can cause untold damage to the one full of it.

> *"Blessed is the man who remains steadfast under trial, for when he has stood the test he will receive the crown of life, which God has promised to those who love him. Let no one say when he is tempted, "I am being tempted by God," for God cannot be tempted with evil, and he himself tempts no one. But each person is tempted when he is lured and enticed by his own desire. Then desire when it has conceived gives birth to sin, and sin when it is fully grown brings forth death.*
> *James 1:12-15 (ESV)*

Nobody is exempt from temptation. If you speak to anyone struggling with addition, they'd most likely tell you that they never expected to become addicted. It crept up on them.

One decision after another formed a negative pattern of behaviour that became too difficult to *just stop*. That's why we need one another. The Israelites grew stronger as they engaged in combat **together**, conquering one territory at a time.

This is not a time to make treaties with the enemy. It is not a time to negotiate with serpents. You are not fighting flesh and blood. *Deuteronomy 7* parallels where we are at, but it is the invisible realm of other gods that you're called to demolish. The Bible clearly defines how we should live and what we should not entertain. It outlines a way of life, but ultimately the absence of God, the lack of Love (God Himself), is sin; walking in our own fleshly desires. Jesus laid His life down as the ultimate sacrifice and demonstration of love to cover sin with His blood. That doesn't give anyone licence to sin or to negotiate what sin is. It does, however, demonstrate that there is a greater love that can cover that sin, where it is acknowledged and repentance sought. We are not here to point the finger, but as brothers and sisters in Christ, we are called to stand alongside each other in unity.

> *"Endeavouring to keep the unity of the*
> *Spirit in the bond of peace".*
> *Ephesians 4:3 (KJV)*

It is time to discern what the Spirit seeks to speak to you.

God is searching for those who hear the call and respond with radical faith. Even stepping out and doing it afraid.

I was an insecure child who grew up conditioned to put on a mask, therefore hiding my true insecurities. For years, I would not step out of my comfort zone for fear of negative consequences. But after finding faith in my Saviour, I learnt how to lean on Him, despite at times, experiencing paralysing fear. I learned to **do it afraid**. The choice was often, sink or swim. Despite shaking inwardly, I've had to do this in all kinds of circumstances, such as speaking from large stages, meeting with prominent figures, or performing job roles I felt ill-equipped for, even in seemingly insignificant situations that sought to immobilise me through fear, the faithfulness of God has proved sure and certain.

Gideon is recognised as one of the great heroes of the Bible, but did you know he did it afraid? When God told him to tear down the Baal altar and Asherah pole, he did it at night because he was so afraid of his family and the townspeople. Nevertheless, he obeyed God and was faithful to the call *Judges 6:27*. Interestingly, when the angel first appeared to Gideon, he said,

> *"The Lord is with you, mighty warrior."*
> *Judges 6:12, (NIV)*

God knew how fearful he was, yet sent the angel to declare who he would become. Consider perhaps how God sees you, or those around you. Not as you are, but what you (or they) will become. *Judges 7* then offers us an exciting account of how God stripped an already frightened young Gideon down to just three hundred men. The Lord removed any reliance he may have had in his own abilities, winning the battle with just a few trumpets and empty jars, gave God the glory.

It is time to discern how to stand together. But together under the direction of our great Commander, who already knows what the future holds and how the victory will outplay.

We can learn a healthy lesson from the redwood.

I have long had a particular affection for redwood trees. They have a beauty, strength, and grandeur to be admired. Interestingly, I was given a prophetic drawing of the trunk of one such tree. The artist then told me what God showed them through the picture. They began by sharing that they saw me dancing around this tree. The artist didn't know I was a dancer, nor the fact about my fascination with redwoods. The word she gave me isn't relevant here, but I want to share something awesome about redwood trees with you. To clarify: I am not a tree hugger, as my friend suggested, haha, but I stand in awe of God's creation!

The height and statue of the redwood is immense. It is one of the tallest trees on our planet, reaching heights of well over 300 feet. One of the powers of their strength is actually in their root system. Yet did you know that their roots are only 5-6 feet deep. That's pretty shallow when you consider many live over 2,000 and some as much as 3,000 years old, especially since there are much shorter trees with roots that go hundreds of feet into the earth. How can the redwood stand so high and so strong for so long, with roots that only go down a few feet deep? The answer is that they find their anchorage in another way. A redwood tree's roots connect and entwine with the roots of the other trees around it. The secret of their strength is in their connection.

What a powerful lesson that teaches us.

You can grow stronger and stand resilient against the elements by connecting and joining your roots with others in the body of Christ. Together we stand strong. I love how God uses His creation to demonstrate how we should live.

JOURNAL YOUR THOUGHTS

BIBLE

PRAYER

13 ~

Chapter 13

LION OF JUDAH

Many of the words in this book have been written over a period of time and were never intended to be collated in this way. Yet in September 2022, I felt the weight of the Lord pressing an urgency in my spirit, compelling me to write this book with a call, to arise and discern the time.

Let me uncover the mystery of this book's cover.

The quest of compiling this book has been an interesting journey. I thought I knew exactly what to write, but during the process, I experienced the true writer of this work directing me. One afternoon, whilst sitting at my computer poised to write a new chapter, I felt led to create the book's cover. I knew the title of the book and the message it would carry, but didn't know how to convey that on the front cover. As you know, **a book is judged by its cover.**

On opening up the software, I was given a vision of what the cover should look like. I replicated what I saw in my mind, with certain aspects revealing themself as I worked. However, I didn't realise the significance of it at the time.

This chapter unlocks what the Holy Spirit communicated to me only **after** I'd completed the book cover design. I am in awe of how God knew the significance of the cover before I did. **This is the message behind the image.**

As Christians, we often use the symbolic image of a lion in reference to Jesus. Famously, C.S. Lewis alludes to this in his Narnia series, with the character Aslan, the lion, who's identified as a king. But, there is much more to this amazing title. Before I explain the important message behind the cover, there needs to be some anchoring about the Lion of Judah first. The Lion of Judah signifies a **time.** There are only three key references to the Lion of Judah in scripture. One at the beginning, one in the middle, and one at the end of the Bible.

It is in *Genesis*, the *first* book of the Bible that the Lion of Judah is introduced. In *chapter 49* Jacob prophesies over each of his sons who will become the tribes of Israel. He explicitly tells them what will happen to them in the future, see *verse 1*. To Judah he declares,

> *"You are a lion's cub Judah"*
> *Genesis 49:10.*

This is why the symbol of the tribe of Judah is a lion, hence the introduction to the **Lion of Judah**. However, if you dig a little further, you can see a clear reference and prophetic utterance linking the scripture to the coming Messiah, Jesus. Firstly, Jacob declares that Judah's brothers will praise him and bow down to him v8, but then he proclaims:

"The scepter will not depart from Judah,
nor the ruler's staff from between his feet,
until he to whom it belongs shall come and
the obedience of the nations shall be his."
Genesis 49:10 (NIV)

The sceptre (UK spelling) obviously indicates some kind of ruling royalty or monarch, with all nations under him. This inference is then confirmed in *Revelation*, the **last** book of the Bible.

"Then one of the elders said to me, "Do
*not weep! See, the **Lion of the tribe of***
***Judah**, the Root of David, has triumphed.*
He is able to open the scroll and its seven
seals." Then I saw a Lamb, looking as if it
had been slain, standing at the center of the
throne, encircled by the four living creatures
and the elders...."
Revelation 5:5-6 (NIV)

Here we see that only the Lion of Judah is able to open the scroll. At the centre of the throne (royalty) is the **Lamb** who was slain. And it is the Lamb that takes the scroll and opens it. The Lamb who was slain and shed his blood to purchase God's people from every tribe and nation.

"You are worthy to take the scroll and to
open its seals, because you were slain, and
***with your blood** you purchased for God*
persons from every tribe and language and
people and nation. You have made them to
be a kingdom and priests to serve our God,
and they will reign on the earth."
Revelation 5:9-10 (NIV)

Wow, just wow!

The Bible begins and ends with the Lion of Judah. The Lamb is the Lion of Judah. He is

> *"the Alpha and the Omega, the First and*
> *the Last, the Beginning and the End."*
> *Revelation 22:13 (NIV)*

- From first to last - Genesis to Revelation.

The image on the cover has the lion's eye highlighted in colour to signify that **God wants you to see what He sees.** He alone, by His Spirit, can truly reveal everything that He wants to show you and speak to you. It is time for your purpose to unfold, but we often only see in part. The front cover reveals half of the lion, and the back cover, the other half. Only when you put the two sides together can you see a complete picture (albeit underneath the text).

Let me tell you a story...

Once upon a time there were two brothers. The eldest brother was born into a royal household with loving parents. His father raised him within the strict boundaries of their law, teaching him everything he needed to know about the rules and customs of their land. This son obeyed his father unquestioningly and observed what he had been taught. The younger son, unlike his older brother, wasn't born into the royal family. He was rescued as a child from an illegitimate background, and adopted. Nevertheless, he was brought up with the same love and acceptance the parents had shown their first born. Since experiencing the hardship of life, the adopted son quickly embraced the acceptance and unconditional love that was lavished on him.

As they each grew older, both the sons presented different challenges. The eldest son knew that he was of the bloodline. He knew his entitlement, but he became legalistic about traditions and practices, shaming his brother who didn't always follow them. Despite making many mistakes, the youngest son continued to be forgiven and embraced. This only angered the eldest brother who became indignant towards the youngest, denying that he was part of the family.

The adopted one, however, knew that his parents accepted him for who he was. He understood that he didn't need to perform to gain his father's approval; he was unconditionally loved. However, this son was often irreverent to his father. He often didn't demonstrate the level of respect that was due to his family, taking his inheritance for granted.

The eldest brother was full of legalism and entitlement, whilst in contrast the youngest brother was often reckless and lacking in honour. *I'll unpack this more a bit later.* The story reminds us that two members of the same family can have two totally different views of their parents. This may be because they were born at different periods in time, so the situation and circumstance in which they are raised is not identical. Yet the parents are the same and their love for their children shouldn't be any different.

In this scenario, it is possible to recognise ourselves. Do you see yourself as the older brother with the birthright, or the younger sibling who can get away with almost anything? As Christians, we can potentially align with both of these. I have certainly seen both mindsets within churches, and myself. That is food for thought.

Whatever the case, you may recognise the parallel here that this story is attempting to highlight. In *Genesis*, the **Lion of Judah** was identified within Israel, and in Revelation is revealed as the Christ (the Lamb of God) who shed His blood for sinners. Jesus received the punishment we deserved for our sin and took it in our place. By grace we are saved by the Lion of Judah.

Before we move on, let me share the third place that a lion and Judah are mentioned together, in the *middle* of the Bible.

> *"For I will be like a lion to Ephraim, like*
> *a great lion to Judah. I will tear them to*
> *pieces and go away; I will carry them off,*
> *with no one to rescue them. Then I will*
> *return to my lair until they have borne their*
> *guilt and seek my face— in their misery*
> *they will earnestly seek me."*
> *Hosea 5:14-15 (NIV)*

That is a tough scripture. Here, Ephraim and Judah represent Israel, (Ephraim was one of Joseph's sons and is often used to identify the ten northern tribes of Israel). Here, God is angry with their idolatry and disobedience, so much so that He describes coming as a lion to tear and carry them off, until they repent and earnestly seek Him. Israel here is being punished for their disobedience. We, however, have been forgiven, by grace. Two brothers of one Father: one by royal birthright and the other by adoption. In *John 15:5* Jesus tells us that He is the vine and we are the branches.

> *"If some of the branches have been broken*
> *off, and you, though a wild olive shoot,*

have been grafted in among the others and now share in the nourishing sap from the olive root, do not consider yourself to be superior to those other branches. If you do, consider this: You do not support the root, but the root supports you. You will say then, "Branches were broken off so that I could be grafted in." Granted. But they were broken off because of unbelief, and you stand by faith. Do not be arrogant, but tremble. For if God did not spare the natural branches, he will not spare you either."
Romans 11:17-21 (NIV)

We need to remember that because of **His grace**, God has lovingly grafted us into the vine whilst others have been broken off because they rebelled. But just because God disciplined Israel doesn't mean that He won't show them just as much mercy if they recognise Him as their Messiah. The Jews are God's sons of the birthright and we are the adopted ones, loved, cherished, forgiven, accepted. Lest we forget, it's important to recognise that God made a covenant with Abram (later named Abraham). This was a promise to make him into the great nation of Israel, and to bless his descendants.

"I will make you into a great nation, and I will bless you; I will make your name great, and you will be a blessing. I will bless those who bless you, and whoever curses you I will curse; and all peoples on earth will be blessed through you."
Genesis 12: 2-3 (NIV)

This covenant is a binding promise that cannot be broken, because God cannot lie, *Hebrews 6: 17-18*. As it says in *Hebrews*, God confirmed it with an oath. An unbreakable contract of love from the Father to His son. Therefore, this covenant stands today, as an everlasting promise. However, *Hebrews* continues to expand and explain that Jesus made the way for **a New Covenant**. This is not a replacement, but an improvement. Or perhaps it is better described as the update God always had planned. However, our hardware wasn't ready for it when God originally created it. Those who accept the sacrifice that Jesus made for us on the cross, can reap the benefits of this eternal promise.

> *"Because of this oath, Jesus has become the guarantor of a better covenant."*
> *Hebrews 7:22 (NIV)*

Jeremiah 31:33-35 (NIV) prepares the way for the new covenant, explaining that God would put His law in the minds and write it on their hearts. It opens a new door to knowing the Lord, as we now know by His Holy Spirit that was sent because of Christ's resurrection. The receiving of the forgiveness of our sins by His blood shed once and for all, as opposed to the ritualistic animal sacrifices. But the new covenant does not nullify the old, which promises an inheritance for Israel. There is a warning to learn from Israel's error, so that we can continue in His kindness.

> *"Consider therefore the kindness and sternness of God: sternness to those who fell, but kindness to you, provided that you continue in his kindness. Otherwise, you also will be cut off. And if they do not persist in unbelief, they will be grafted in, for God is able to graft them in again. After*

all, if you were cut out of an olive tree that is wild by nature, and contrary to nature were grafted into a cultivated olive tree, how much more readily will these, the natural branches, be grafted into their own olive tree."
Romans 11:22-24 (NIV)

Just like the story of the prodigal son in *Luke 15*, we need to **carry the heart of the Father** to all those who have been led astray and wandered from the path. This is the time for the prodigals (Jew and Gentile) to be welcomed back into the fold. God is calling you to align with your brother (and sister!). We are seated on two separate sides (just like the book cover) of the Father heart of God. One side recognises the reverence and authority, the other the grace and mercy. **Both need to be aligned in this time.**

Be careful not to judge what you don't understand.
May you discern what He is speaking and your response to His call for unity.

I was told emphatically that an author should never design their own book cover. It is important to get another professional to design it, but although it appears I ignored the advice, in truth, I didn't design it - the Creator of all gave me a download because He had a message that I was unaware of. He wants to convey it to you. So, be watchful not to disregard what God is speaking.

JOURNAL YOUR THOUGHTS

BIBLE

PRAYER

14 ~

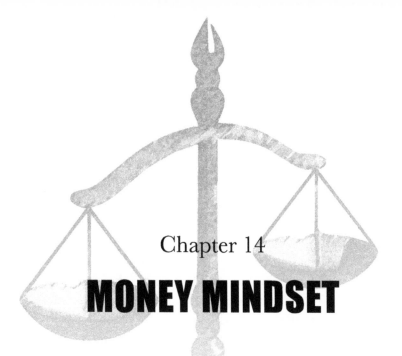

Chapter 14

MONEY MINDSET

Money makes the world go around, or so the Liza Minnelli song from Cabaret would have you believe.

"It doesn't matter about money; having it, not having it. Or having clothes, or not having them. You're still left alone with yourself in the end." *Billy Idol (singer)*

"Too many people spend money they earned..to buy things they don't want..to impress people that they don't like." *Will Rogers (vaudeville performer, actor & commentator)*

Those comments may or may not resonate with you. A quick Internet search will offer you hundreds of quotes about money. It seems the world is fixated with it and everyone has their favourite little saying about it. A slogan that becomes a personal motto. From those who announce that they have more weeks than money at the end of the month, to those who attempt to remind themselves that money isn't everything. Certainly, some of these phrases have elements of positive inspiration, but for many the answer may be, "that's all very well, but in the words of Jerry Maguire *(an old film)* "show me the money!"

People are obsessed with money. So, this book would not be complete with regards to discerning the time, if it isn't addressed. In fact, this is perhaps the most difficult chapter to write, since I am aware that the topic of money raises emotive responses. In many ways, this chapter is not so much about the matter of money, but the **matter of the heart.** When you poke someone's heart, you will get a response. **Money helps you get to the heart of the matter -** to see what is within you. As the scripture below highlights, it will disclose where your true treasure lies.

> *"Do not store up for yourselves treasures on earth, where moths and vermin destroy, and where thieves break in and steal. But store up for yourselves treasures in heaven, where moths and vermin do not destroy, and where thieves do not break in and steal. For where your treasure is, there your heart will be also."*
> *Matthew 6:19-21 (NIV)*

Matthew reminds us here that this world is passing. If your investment is in trying to build your mansion on earth, then when it is suddenly swept away, what will you have left? Jesus doesn't say you can't have a mansion, but He does say, where your treasure is, there your heart will be also. Where is your treasure?

How do you know your own heart?

Jeremiah reminds us that the Lord searches our hearts and examines the mind. You can ask the Holy Spirit to reveal your own heart to you, since the prophet also reminds us that we can deceive ourselves. Your mind is often led by your heart, so consider where your thoughts go? What do you find yourself daydreaming about? What hidden longings do you carry that nobody else sees? Our words, too, reveal much about what is going on in our hearts. Consciously listen to your own words for any clues about what is hidden in your heart.

> *"The heart is deceitful above all things and beyond cure. Who can understand it? 'I the Lord search the heart and examine the mind, to reward each person according to their conduct, according to what their deeds deserve.'"*
> *Jeremiah 17: 9-10 (NIV)*

During my late teens and early twenties, I struggled with an eating disorder, a typical consequence for a dancer emerging from childhood trauma. In the dance studios we were surrounded by mirrors, having to assess our posture and movement during our daily classes. Analysing my own body became an obsession. Constantly comparing myself to others and the glamour models in magazines only fuelled my preoccupation with my body and, consequently, food. After surrendering my life to God, He began to walk me through a journey of healing and victory. Most of this involved the Lord realigning my thinking as He brought me revelations of His love. However, in the midst of this process, I was horrified by the uncovering of my own heart. The Holy Spirit showed me how my mind was consumed with thoughts about my body and food. I struggled with body dysmorphia, where perceptions of my body shape were warped. He spoke gently, but firmly, about the idolatry hidden in my heart. My body and food so absorbed my thoughtlife that they were in competition with God Himself. He alone needs to be on the throne of our hearts. I learnt a humbling lesson about the subtlety of **where my treasure had been placed.**

However, at the time, I didn't recognise I also had an unhealthy mindset regarding money.

Over the years I've had friendships with people who've had literally nothing, many who were living on the streets. I've also known those classed as millionaires who can access money and do virtually anything they want with money. The majority of people I know, however, fall somewhere in the broad spectrum between. When we lived in a two bedroom flat with three young children, I remember feeling like the poor relation compared to some of my friends in our middle class neighbourhood. Yet, at the same time, I felt embarrassed when we got a new car or went on a nice holiday. The car was second-hand and the holiday was cheap, but as we knew people who were struggling to put food on the table, I was ashamed. On the one hand I was consumed with guilt knowing some people watched our lives jealousy. Yet simultaneously, on the other hand, I was full of envy watching others who lived in their large detached homes with massive gardens with expensive cars and holidays. *Note,* I carried both shame and envy in my heart.

At that time, I also believed I was content with little. To a degree I was, but the lack of money over the years had actually brought about a poverty mentality. We'd lived through a time when the tins in our cupboard were colour-coordinated blue and white. A well-known supermarket's value products all came in the same packaging. You just needed to be careful to read the label before opening, so you didn't end up with tinned peaches on your toast instead of baked beans! We laugh about it now, but this is why I felt guilty when I had money. I'd heard sermons that suggested money equalled selfishness and Jesus was poor, so we should be too. Yet, as I studied the Word and grew in my relationship with the Lord, I discovered a loving Father who delighted in giving me good gifts. God showed me that the entire earth belongs to Him and from it comes every jewel, mineral, and source of fuel. The earth is full of wealth and Our Father owns it all. But **money is not the indicator by which our worth is measured.** If God so choses, He can release it to whom He pleases. But He is more concerned with the health of your heart than your comfort. Let that sink in.

What I hadn't understood was that I judged those who had money and was frustrated with God for withholding it from me. Yet, He allowed my lack to bring me to my knees, where I learnt about His faithfulness.

Being on stage, I was constantly in the public eye. At the age of twenty-one, I lived alone in an annexed apartment. It was basic, but a perfect first rental. My grandma taught me how to utilise what I had in my hands and I put my creative improvisational skills to work. Brought up during war time, she'd gained some invaluable skills. My mother, as a single parent for many years, also taught me to *survive* by taking one day at a time. She taught herself DIY because she had no other option. Having learnt these lessons from them both, I built my own wardrobe, using a rod and curtain, sewed cushions, re-painted a coffee table and much more.

During that period, God miraculously provided me with a practically new car and my signature leather jacket. Both came by the hand of God, yet when it came to food and bills, I barely scraped by each month. It was very stressful at times, but I learnt how to lean into the Father and trust that He would provide. Outwardly, driving my shiny car, wearing my leather jacket, and performing on stage probably looked as if I had money. That is the impression some people had of me. However, when I was alone in my apartment on my face before God, seeking Him for all that I needed, and having to forgive those who judged me, **I found gold**. A treasure that is beyond monetary value. Communion with my Father in Heaven, worth so much more.

When searching the heart and listening to the conversation in our heads, as I mentioned earlier, the subject of money seems to bring out strong emotive reactions. It is helpful to recognise why that is. What makes you feel angry, or frustrated, or whatever else, when you think of money? Most people mention injustices. 'Unfair' is a word commonly used. It is time to search your heart to allow God to bring to the surface any misalignment. I see many sitting in judgement of others because of money: the lack of it, the abundance of it, the use of it, the appearance of it.

> *"For the love of money is a root of all kinds*
> *of evil, for which some have strayed from*
> *the faith in their greediness, and pierced*
> *themselves through with many sorrows."*
> *1 Timothy 6:10 (NKJV)*

Money in itself is not evil. The love of it, however, will draw you away from God. Is your heart and mind set on money or what money can buy? Does your heart desire things, or maybe popularity and status? Those are the areas that can subtly draw your attention away from what is of real importance. Sometimes, our motives can seem good to ourselves and others. But false humility and pride can hide if you don't constantly address the state of your own heart.

Allow yourself to be completely honest, so that you can bare your heart before the Lord. He has such a wealth of treasure for you. It may take many forms. Do not despise those who receive financial wealth, nor condemn those who have lack, but desire the **greater riches** that stem from the fruits of the Spirit. Desire not to be known so much by others, but to know the One who is the true influencer of life.

How do you know if you have an issue with money?

By the control you give it. Do you feel as if your life is controlled by money? Are the decisions you make based solely on your finances? Many of you have known what it is to struggle financially, but as I said earlier, it is all relative. "I can't afford to ..." is a phrase I've heard *and used* all too often. God taught me if I'd waited until I could afford to get married, have children, or move out of our flat, it probably would never have happened. As we obeyed, so God provided. I am not condoning the famous tagline, "Just do it", but rather encouraging you to step out when God speaks.

Do you have any miraculous testimonies? I am privileged to have known a few incredible people who believed against all odds. Called to set up different types of residential training centres costing several millions of pounds, each of them believed that God would provide what He promised them. Despite not seeing God's provision when they expected it, even when others around them gave up hope, they held on by faith. **They believed that He is faithful**.

Each of their faith projects resulted in thousands of people being impacted through their different ministries. These were regular people who didn't have money, but they did possess extraordinary faith. Their motives didn't hide a secret agenda, but their hearts led to a generation discipled for the Kingdom. God will often allow impossible situations to provide opportunities for the miraculous. The journey was tough and most people don't know what it cost them personally (and I don't just mean financially). They stood against the odds, on the Word they'd been given.

If everything came easy, we'd be tempted to take the credit ourselves. Let's not forget, God loves us too much to give us what we cannot handle. He alone deserves the glory.

> *"He led you through the vast and dreadful*
> *wilderness, that thirsty and waterless land,*
> *with its venomous snakes and scorpions.*
> *He brought you water out of hard rock. He*
> *gave you manna to eat in the wilderness,*
> *something your ancestors had never known,*
> *to humble and test you so that in the end*
> *it might go well with you. You may say to*
> *yourself, 'My power and the strength of my*
> *hands have produced this wealth for me.'*
> *But remember the Lord your God, for it is he*
> *who gives you the ability to produce wealth,*
> *and so confirms his covenant, which he*
> *swore to your ancestors, as it is today."*
> *Deuteronomy 8:15-18 (NIV)*

If you step back, you'll remember that money in itself has little, if any, value. It is a piece of paper or coin that **represents value.**

Have you ever watched any of those shipwreck or plane crash programmes that leave its passengers stranded on a desert island? The characters are typically classes of various kinds of people from a range of backgrounds. What quickly emerges is a quick levelling or reshuffling of value. The stereotypes often have the high achieving office worker or wealthy business person that doesn't necessarily have the skills needed to survive on a remote island. It is typically the tradesman or manual labourer who has the strength and skills to provide shelter and hunt for food. Survival is what is needed. Money becomes worthless.

The story of the brothers, Esau and Jacob, highlights this point.When Esau arrived home hungry one day, he sold his birthright to his brother Jacob for some of the stew he was cooking. At the time Esau's hunger overtook the importance of his birthright. This is what the scripture tells us when he spoke to Jacob,

> *"'Look, I am about to die' Esau said.*
> *'What good is the birthright to me?'"*
> *Genesis 25:32 (NIV).*

This passage emphasises the value not of money, but of the **exchange.** Again, take a look at the following scripture. In context, you can see that when the Egyptians ran out of money, they had to look at alternative ways to trade for food.

> *"'Then bring your livestock,' said Joseph.*
> *'I will sell you food in exchange for your*

livestock, since your money is gone.'"
Genesis 47:16 (NIV)

Money is a universally recognised means of creating **a transaction**. An agreement of exchange. You may not have what the person you are trading with wants, so you use money that can then be exchanged for anything. Not everyone uses money. Many countries still barter with livestock or other goods in exchange for what they want.

Let me tell you funny story:

On a holiday in Tunisia, a female friend and I were together when a vendor drew us into a conversation. He had apparently spotted me and wanted to marry me! Despite explaining that I was already married, (my husband was with the children at the time), he began to barter for me. After offering to give my husband a camel in exchange for me, he then upped the offer to two camels! Finally, he asked, "Well then, how many camels would he want?" You may laugh, but the seller was quite serious. Thankfully, my husband was not there to accept his offer! I may think I am worth more (certainly to my husband) than a couple of camels, but the value is decided by the one willing to pay.

These days more people are investing in crypto currency. This is not just a digital version of money. It is more about the transaction that is captured through a chain of digital records called blockchain. The blockchain identifies the sale and ownership via the digital chain of data created in the transaction. The advantage of this is that it is given a timestamp and unique set of information that cannot be altered or deleted. Much (though not all) crypto currency is also decentralised, meaning that it is not controlled by governments or central authorities. These technologies enable peer to peer connections that eradicate the need for banks or mediators, so that you can do direct business with each other.

I am not encouraging you to embrace nor disregard digital currencies, it is just a fact. It is important that you are aware of the changes that are happening around us. Many of these digital technologies have been around for years. It is just that they are now becoming more visible and accessible to the mainstream. **It is not to fear, but to discern**. God is Lord of all and is in all. It is time to be vigilant.

> *"Therefore I tell you, do not worry about your life, what you will eat or drink; or about your body, what you will wear. Is not life more than food, and the body more than clothes? Look at the birds of the air; they do not sow or reap or store away in barns, and yet your heavenly Father feeds them. Are you not much more valuable than they? Can any one of you by worrying add a single hour to your life?... Therefore do not worry about tomorrow, for tomorrow will worry about itself. Each day has enough trouble of its own."*
> *Matthew 6: 25-34 (NIV)*

There are those who have come from Egypt and those who were born in the wilderness, but we are all to cross over into the **promised land,** and into everything that God has for us. There are those who are of the digital native generation, and those who are the Joshua and Caleb generation who will help to lead them, with wisdom gained in the wilderness. Whichever generation you fit in, you are called to be among them, so it is essential that you recognise your place. I will expand on this in another chapter. For now, I want to share the word that God put in my spirit over a couple of years ago. Let me first, bring some context through my own testimony.

For many years I learnt to thrive in the wilderness. I experienced miracle after miracle of God's provision. The majority of the time, the provision wasn't what I expected. It didn't usually come through the traditional means and wasn't necessarily what I wanted. Nevertheless, I grew to experience what it is to rely daily on the **manna from Heaven**, the manifestation of provision in a vast variety of ways. As I mentioned earlier, I received a miracle car. In fact, God has provided two miracle cars. Each was provided through completely different means. Nobody knew my need, but the Father did.

At one time we opened our home for a family to live with us, because they had nowhere to go. One of the results from this time was that my washing machine broke after so much use. The microwave I'd been grateful for, was my grandma's old one and that didn't last either, and our cooker took twice as long as it should to cook anything. During this time, we'd used all of our resources, so I sought the Lord for His guidance, since I was not looking forward to more trips to the launderette. I was led to an email offering the opportunity to review products in exchange for them. Within weeks my entire kitchen was kitted out with brand new appliances. Three months later, the review process was scrapped. I was offered the opportunity at the exact time my family needed them.

That was a miracle that brought me to my knees in gratitude.

But did you know that God likes to show up in the details, and have fun in doing so... Whilst walking down the high street one day, a sealed card appeared at my feet. It was lying there upside down in its wrapper, unopened. There were numerous shoppers busily passing by, oblivious to what was on the floor. It would have been impossible to find the original owner, but picking it up and turning it over revealed that it was a birthday card. That day was my birthday and I hadn't received any cards, at that point. As I read it, I could hear the Father saying, "Happy Birthday, Sarah", with a big smile on his face and laughter in His eyes, as it brought a tear to mine. These are just a few examples. I've experienced some extreme hardship and some awesome blessings, but through it all, I've known God's hand at work in both the large and small miracles. I love where, especially in the little things, He demonstrates how He knows us completely, *Psalm 139*.

As I share the word God laid on my heart, let Him speak to your spirit, so that you can **discern what He is saying to you personally.** Maybe you relate to receiving manna from Heaven - God's timely provision. Note that you only receive a miracle when you are in a position where you need one. It is a stretching, training, and growing experience. Through this humbling experience the Israelites learnt to rely on God through the wilderness. As they walked for forty years in the desert, they had no means of providing for themselves. They learnt about the Lord's faithfulness, they experienced water from a rock, manna, quail, and clothes that didn't wear out.

> *"God led you all the way in the wilderness these forty years, to humble and test you in order* **to know what was in your heart,** *whether or not you would keep his*

commands. He humbled you, causing you to
hunger and then feeding you with manna,
which neither you nor your ancestors had
known, to teach you that man does not live
on bread alone but on every word that comes
from the mouth of the Lord. Your clothes
did not wear out and your feet did not swell
during these forty years."
Deuteronomy 8: 2-4 (NIV)

Notice here, God was testing to see what was in their **hearts.** This test is not like an exam to see if you will fail; it is a revealing of what is within. If you test a battery, you want to see how much power it holds, then you know if it is up to the job. God, in His mercy, doesn't want to give you what you can't handle. You only have to take a look at the celebrity culture or lottery winners to see how many didn't handle fame or fortune. If you receive what you're not ready for, you'll forget who your source is. Read that sentence again. The Israelites quickly forgot where their provision came from, let's not do the same. The wilderness years have been to show YOU what is in your heart. To reveal to you where your true affections lie. God is preparing your heart to receive blessings. He is about to pour our supernatural provision and wealth (not just monetary, but for many it will be). In order for this to happen, the manna will need to dry up. This is the season we are in. If you're used to receiving manna, you may have noticed those clothes wearing out and the lack of manna that you've become accustomed to.

This is part of the preparation.

I will go more into the time of preparation in one of the following chapters. But can you discern that this is part of your training? Do you have a sense of expectation?

God wants to bless His people abundantly, as the wilderness years are over and coming to an end. In the Promised Land you will work differently. You will use the skills you learnt back in Egypt. You were trained in the hard place under slavery, but in the open space, you will use what you learnt. I see people building their own houses and tilling their own land without the need for slave masters. Your food will come by your own hand. There will be businesses raised up in the marketplace for those who have solutions to needs in society. **Creative solutions** breathed in the night through dreams or in the early hours, by the breath of God. As you walk or lift your voice in praise, your mind will suddenly see the Creator directing His creation.

The world will begin to look and to notice, to see and to hear. A mighty rush of wind, like the Holy Spirit at Pentecost will come upon new ventures that are led by the Almighty. **Those who hear, who discern and are prepared**, will see the hand of God open in miraculous ways. There will be miraculous open doors opened, provision, and favour. But there will be a cost. Everything has a cost. Friendships, relationships, marriage, children, jobs, all have a cost. Fame has a cost. Wealth has a cost. Your faith has a cost. The cost of denying yourself to follow His lead.

What does that look like?

The Bible teaches us how to keep our hearts soft. In *Genesis 4* you can read about Cain and Abel. The story exemplifies how the heart is searched by the Lord. The brothers both brought an offering to God. Cain brought "some of the fruits" of his labour, whereas his brother Abel brought "the fat portions and some of the firstborn".

In other words, Abel gave God his **best**. The first part of what he had. Unlike Cain, who gave God something, but it wasn't the best he could bring. It was not about whether it was meat or vegetables, but it was about the heart.

> *"In the course of time Cain brought* ***some of the fruits of the soil as an*** ***offering to the Lord.*** *And Abel also brought an offering—****fat portions from*** ***some of the firstborn of his flock.*** *The Lord looked with favour on Abel and his offering, but on Cain and his offering he did not look with favour. So Cain was very angry, and his face was downcast."*
> Genesis 4:3-5 (NIV)

Tithing, which is giving your first fruits to the Lord, helps you to know your own heart. It is less about the amount or what it looks like, and more about the attitude in which it is given. In addition to money, God may lead you to give in other ways, such as tithing your time. Perhaps, He may call on you to offer Him your home, by welcoming in someone in need. Whatever He directs you to, it is how you honour Him in private that He seeks. **Tithes and offerings** are not something to give in order to get back, they should be the **overflow of our heart** in thanksgiving for the faithfulness of God. Are your actions a demonstration of the heart?

> *"These people honor me with their lips, but their hearts are far from me."* Matthew 15:8 (NIV)

Cain was angry because he saw God favour his brother's offering, not realising that the fault was within his own heart. His jealousy led to his downfall. What was the result? He murdered his own brother. As you guard your heart (*Proverbs 4:23*) to allow the Spirit to search it, reveal what is hidden within and heal it, you will be amazed at the joy and fulfilment you will find. No-one can see what is beneath the surface of the exterior you present. But none of us can hide from the omnipotent God who is all knowing. That should bring you reassurance, to know that the Father sees all, yet still loves you unconditionally. And He is helping you to discover that love through the challenges of life, so that you will be equipped to help others. If you see others raised up when you have sacrificed in ways nobody knows, be assured, the Father sees and will reward you.

> *"Let the words of my mouth and the* **meditation of my heart** *Be acceptable in Your sight, O LORD, my rock and my Redeemer."*
> *Psalm 19:14 (NKJV)*

The cost of being a disciple is to deny yourself and take up your cross daily, *Matthew 16:24*. God will pour out an abundance of wealth for those who show themselves faithful stewards.

JOURNAL YOUR THOUGHTS

BIBLE

PRAYER

15 ~

Chapter 15

THE JOSEPH YEARS

The following is a word that's been in my spirit over some time.

For a number of years God has been speaking to me about the feast and famine, saying **the Joseph years** are coming. Like film trailers, the Bible is full of prequels of what's to come. You can see a thread of a beautifully woven tapestry sewn through its pages.

A neighbour of mine is a dressmaker who produces wedding and bridesmaid dresses. However, she doesn't just make them from scratch, she's regularly adjusting the garments, so that they'll fit the bride and her entourage perfectly. My own wedding dress needed considerable adjustments made before I could wear it. It was actually my friend's wedding dress. We'd gone shopping together and I'd helped her choose it. I loved the dress, but never dreamt I'd be walking down the aisle in it, exactly one year later! Since I married quickly, on a thin budget, my friend kindly told me I could use the dress. The only issue was that we were a few sizes apart, in addition to our body shape being completely different. Thankfully, she was happy for my aunt to make some radical changes. In addition to adjusting the size, she did an amazing job. The dress was transformed, with alternative styled sleeves and additional lace around the bodice, but she maintained most of its original pattern and design.

In the same way, I see how the Father has designed patterns through life. **Seasons**, for example, rotate each year but can look completely different each time they come around. Earlier you read about the arks we are to prepare, building on the pattern of Noah. And then the pattern of Moses, journeying from slavery, through the wilderness, and into the promised land. So also, the time of Joseph has resounded in my spirit. Seven years of feast then seven years of famine. This is what Joseph saw when he interpreted Pharaoh's dream.

> *"Seven years of great abundance are coming throughout the land of Egypt, but seven years of famine will follow them. Then all the abundance in Egypt will be forgotten, and the famine will ravage the land. The abundance in the land will not be remembered, because the famine that follows it will be so severe."*
> *Genesis 41: 29-31 (NIV)*

Note that the seven years of famine that ensued wiped out the remembrance of the abundance, just as the tsunami wiped out the previous beaches, which I told you about. Why, then, was Pharaoh given the dream? So that they were prepared. God was warning Pharaoh in advance, in order for him to put preparations in place, so that the Israelites would be saved from the famine that was coming. He then released Joseph from prison and raised him up to oversee the necessary details that would ensure Egypt's survival during the time of famine.

> *"And now let Pharaoh look for a discerning and wise man and put him in charge of the land of Egypt."* verse 33

A discerning person won't be singularly focussed on the time of abundance, but will be shrewdly planning ahead.

Since 2015, God has been speaking to me about a new move of the Spirit. An excitement arose in my spirit during that year with anticipation of what is about to happen. But as I've come to understand, God is outside of our limitations of time.

> *"But do not forget this one thing, dear friends: With the Lord a day is like a thousand years, and a thousand years are like a day. The Lord is not slow in keeping his promise, as some understand slowness. Instead he is patient with you, not wanting anyone to perish, but everyone to come to repentance."*
> *2 Peter 3:8-9 (NIV)*

In the late eighties, early nineties, I was the dancer in a Christian pop band. It was actually much more than a band, we were a prophetic ministry team that toured the UK and abroad, sharing God's heart. We experienced the hand of God on what we did in tremendous ways. To give you some context, we had two songs in the UK

181

pop-charts. *Tears from Heaven,* specifically shared God's heart for the people of our nation, across the airwaves. Doors of opportunity opened as we continued to tell our audiences about the love of God through television, radio, and from stage as we toured. But above that, it was the transformation in the lives of those who flocked to see us that was so powerful. People of all ages, but especially young people and young adults were drawn, not to us, but into a relationship with God. Hundreds would literally run crying to the front of the stage, not to us, but to the altar to receive salvation. Tears streamed as they cried out in repentance and longing for more of Jesus. There were times when we did literally nothing, but watch the power of God at work. Miracles and healings were commonplace.

One of our songs carried a prophetic word about a tidal wave hitting the shores of Britain. The vision was of the Holy Spirit moving in power and transformation across the UK, bringing healing and forgiveness. Nancy Goudie, who headed up the ministry with her late husband Ray, saw this in her spirit and the prophecy was incorporated into the song, *Heal Our Nation.* It may have been written in the 80s, but it is a word for now. It is the song that again has resurfaced in my ears, as I hear God crying out for our land.

A cry for revival.

Yet, I have increasingly sensed an imminent move of the Holy Spirit over recent years. God told me that what I had seen previously was just a tiny **glimpse of what is to come.** Whether you remember that era or not, it is time to allow expectancy to grow. Whether it is a literal seven years, (like with Joseph) or not, I do not know, but there is a time of feast on its way. A time that will blow you away. There will be favour, provision, miracles, and salvations, prodigals returning and those encountering the Lord for the first time. It will be a time that cannot be attributed to man. God alone will be the one who takes the Glory. But there is a warning to discern; **discern the time**, for it will not last.

The time of feasting will be a rich blessing for many, but not everyone will rejoice at what God will do. There will be many who despise and ridicule; those who will seek to undermine what will happen. You should have your eyes and ears open to the Spirit. For there will be a time beyond that; a time of famine. The famine will not necessarily be what you imagine. It will come suddenly and stop many in their tracks. But those who are prepared will know what to do. They will know that their God is for them and will protect them during this time. This book aims to help prepare and equip you with the insight to be ready. To discern the time because no-one can pin down God's exact timing.

How can you keep yourself alert and ready? It requires a continual surrendering of your heart, a constant turning within to allow the Holy One to do a spiritual health check. Allow the Word to illuminate what is hidden and shine out bright.

In 2015, God spoke to me through an image He showed me of Christmas tree lights.

The lights were the old-fashioned type, where if one bulb failed, none of the lights would work. I saw God connecting people through the thread of His Spirit, as they joined together and the individual bulbs underwent their 'spiritual health checks'. Once the final bulb i.e. person, was in place, the power was switched on. Instantly the space lit up.

Suddenly, the world could see the Church. No longer was it a series of tiny individual lights, but a mass of illumination.

> *"In the beginning was the Word, and the Word was with God, and the Word was God. He was with God in the beginning. Through him all things were made; without him nothing was made that has been made. In him was life, and that life was the light of all mankind. **The light shines in the darkness,** and the darkness has not overcome it."*
> *John 1: 1-4 (NIV)*

Jesus Himself is the Word. He is the Word within us and He is the light within us. Together, the body will shine with the radiance of God and many will be drawn to that light. Through us, joined together in unity, the world will see the light. The light will shine and His Name will be glorified.

Can you imagine the power of this?

We can, perhaps, catch a glimpse of what it could look like, if we turn back to another moment in history. In May 1940 there was a display of an incredible example of the power of unity.

Imagine hearing the cries of desperation from people stuck in what seems like a hopeless situation. Fellow human beings stranded, surrounded and under attack by the enemy, unable to run away. What would you do? How helpless would you feel?

It was during the second world war when allied forces from Britain, France, and Belgium were left stranded on the coast of France in a place called Dunkirk that the miracle took place. Code named Operation Dynamo, most of the rescue took place by large Navy ships, but these were unable to get to many of the soldiers who were trapped on the beach. It was anticipated that 20,000-30,000 could be rescued, but around 338,000 were saved that week. It took the heroism of hundreds of civilians to brave the dangerous waters in their "little ships", such as fishing boats and other small craft, to help evacuate them. The troops were rescued by civilians who were not trained for battle, but who gave little thought to their own safety, to help save the lives of others. A handful of these boats could not have succeeded, but joining together for the common good, resulted in a ray of hope being radiated to the world.

So, too, the time will come when brothers and sisters will arise out of their dormancy, to hear the cries of those in bondage and slavery, to see beyond their own lives. Then there will be a coming together in the body, for the world to see Christ Our King through the Church united in love and service. For unity commands a blessing, *Psalm 133*. This is the strategy of Heaven.

> *"I have given them the glory that you gave me, that they may be one as we are one— I in them and you in me—so that they may be brought to complete unity.* **Then the world will know that you sent me** *and have loved them even as you have loved me."*
> *John 17: 22-23 (NIV)*

As the Church is united, the blessings will fall, and there will be an abundance. There will be gifts from the Father to accomplish His will and because of His great love.

What do you do when you receive a gift? When I was a child, I remember having to write what seemed like an unending stream of thank-you letters. They weren't just short notes with a couple of lines, but information about how their present had blessed me and how grateful I was for their thoughtfulness. It taught me not to take others for granted. To understand that they had thought of me and specifically gone out of their way to demonstrate that. It is important that we too, as God's children, take time to thank Him and give the credit back to where it belongs.

When you fail to give credit back to God for what you receive, it is taken away.

> *"Be careful that you do not forget the Lord your God, failing to observe his commands, his laws and his decrees that I am giving you this day. Otherwise, when you eat and are satisfied, when you build fine houses and settle down, and when your herds and flocks grow large and your silver and gold increase and all you have is multiplied, who brought you out of Egypt, out of the land of slavery, then your heart will become proud and you will forget the Lord your God, who brought you out of Egypt, out of the land of slavery."*
> *Deuteronomy 8:11-14 (NIV)*

Remember Joseph. When the blessings fall, the warning is not to allow your comfort, or increase, make you blind to the following season. Seasons come and go, and the time that will be, will also pass. As will Heaven and earth, but God's Word will remain, *Luke 21:33.*

"Therefore keep watch, because you do not know on what day your Lord will come."
Matthew 24:42 (NIV)

Let us discern.

JOURNAL YOUR THOUGHTS

BIBLE

PRAYER

16 ~

Chapter 16

TIME OF POSITIONING

This part of a word God spoke to me in 2015

This is just some of the word that I wrote down all those years ago, since I don't feel it appropriate to share it in its entirety here. Allow the Holy Spirit to give you insight to hear what He would speak to you through it and allow yourself to apply anything that He shows you:

> When Moses was up Mount Sinai speaking to the Lord, the people stirred up dissatisfaction. They began to moan and grumble to Aaron. Seeking something to guide them, they built a gold calf, and they worshipped the idol. They gave themselves to that which is created, as opposed to the Creator, *Exodus 32*.

> They believed the lie... And so, it began.

Corruption of the mind

The world is living a lie.
You lie to yourselves.
You lie to one another.
And now you believe your own lie.
No longer do you hide your sin behind closed doors, but you parade it in the open, in the daylight. You shine your sin as if it is to be something you are proud of. It has become your stumbling block.

> *"Every way of a man is right in his own eyes; But God weighs the hearts." Proverbs 21:2 (KJV)*

I am coming. I am coming for that which is Mine. I will return to take back, to restore, to heal, to redeem, and to reclaim that which has been stolen from Me.

For you have called that which is sin, as if it were not sin. You have called it by a name that is not sin, to cover your iniquity and to hide your shame. But I am coming to expose that which is sin, and to expose your shame. For you have brought this shame upon yourselves, as you have indulged in that which is SIN.

Go each of you into your own homes and examine your own heart. Open your eyes and see clearly, not through the fog of self-deception. Be bold enough to call that, by which you have deceived yourselves, the rightful name it deserves. Explore the sin within your heart, and repent. Repent and turn away from your sin.

"The spirit of man is the lamp of the Lord, searching all the innermost parts." Proverbs 20:27 (KJV)

Over time, nations have grown in knowledge and understanding, as they have gained insight into their environment and the universe around them, in the name of science. However, in fathoming certain mysteries they have become proud, boasting in their knowledge and believing their skill to be their own. Talent and expertise are words too often applied to an individual or group to applaud their competence. Yet, it is forgotten that each talent is a gift imparted from God above, the only true Creator and life giver.

Technological and scientific advancements hide a chasm of immorality. Pride covers their hearts and blinds their minds. Those with eloquent tongues dull the minds of the ignorant. Comatosed in their unconscious unknowing, these unsuspecting sheep are easily incensed, responding to the sensualised. People move in pack-like formation, seeking to expunge their feelings in a cathartic manner; not only through violence, media, sex, drugs, and so forth, but also in the subtleties of events such as rallies and protests, or conferences that seek to empower *(the flesh)*.

In these environments the power of suggestion is given. Here is the replication down through history of the original deceit, when the serpent taunted Eve with the lie. So too, here, as with Eve, desire is stirred. The flesh comes to life and is enticed.

193

"..For God knows that when you eat
of it [the fruit], your eyes will be
opened, and you will be like God,
knowing good and evil."
Genesis 3:5 (NIV)

Justification and logical explanations will not bear life.

Life, in its essence, cannot be without the One who is Life. And yet there is a counterfeit that will be presented to the world as if it were the ultimate achievement of humankind. So, too, there are coming falsifiers that will deceive. There are plans to play god with the mind, intent that appears to justify its use to change human behaviour for the good. But no man is good, except by the Spirit of God. True discernment is only what will bring clarity to the confusion of what is real and what is false. Technology is being, and has been, developed that would cause an illusion of the truth.

It is time to watch and discern.

That word flowed quickly as I wrote it, and I could sense the power of what God was showing me. There is an urgency in the warning to be alert. It is not to cause fear, but to encourage us to have **your eyes and ears open**. To be fully aware of the time we live in.

We are called to live by the Spirit.

It is easy to feel intimidated by what is happening around us. As Christians, we sometimes want to bury our head in the sand, to hide from things we don't understand and that can seem overwhelming. Yet we are called to stand and not faint. *Hebrews 12* is full of rich encouragement to anyone who is struggling with sin or perseverance in this journey of life. It also encourages us that:

> *"No discipline seems pleasant at the time,*
> *but painful. Later on, however, it produces a*
> *harvest of righteousness and peace for those*
> *who have been trained by it."*
> *Hebrews 12: 11 (NIV)*

It is easy to question why God allows things to happen, but the following may help to put things into perspective as we continue on this journey to discern the times we are living in.

For He surely allows us to go through trials that reveal our own hearts to us. To allow us to see, if we will walk in alignment with the truth that we preach. Do we walk in that forgiveness, humility, and love? Press *pause* for a moment and let the Holy Spirit touch that part in you that you don't want to face. Let Him bring **His light** into any dark area.

> *"My grace is sufficient for you, for My*
> *strength is made perfect in weakness."*
> *2 Corinthians 12:9 (NKJV)*

> *"Let no debt remain outstanding, except*
> *the continuing debt to love one another..."*
> *Romans 13:8 (NIV)*

Do you recognise your brother or sister? Does an ear recognise the heart? A mouth, an ankle? Is it only other parts of the face, hands and feet you align with? What about the veins and capillaries, those hidden yet essential parts that carry the blood to every organ within the body?

God spoke to me about the body, whilst I was directing a local *churches together* project that sought to bring the story of Easter alive in our community. We needed an array of cast and crew to help make it happen. We worked closely with local council, businesses, and members of the public, in addition to church members. God highlighted to me how every church was strategic to its success. Not every church had people capable of acting, or taking on a behind the scenes role, but yet He told me that each one was necessary. The Lord then began speaking to me about **shoulders**. I'd never contemplated shoulders before. But over the pursuing weeks of rehearsals, I couldn't stop being acutely aware of this part of the body. That almost insignificant part of your body that gets little acknowledgment between the head, neck and arms. Yet, the shoulders carry burdens and yokes no other part of the body could bear.

> *"For to us a child is born, to us a son is given, and the government will be on his shoulders." Isaiah 9:6 (NIV)*

Note here that *verse 4* talks of the breaking of the yoke, prior to Jesus' birth. Then it continues to explain that it is His Government, of which there will be no end. *Isaiah 9:7*

This highlights the huge responsibility carried upon the shoulders. But not only do they bear the weight of responsibility, they are also identified as carrying that which is Holy. The names of the sons of Israel were engraved on stones fastened on the shoulder pieces of the ephod as memorial stones. Both *Exodus 28:12 (NIV)* and *Numbers 7:9 (KJV)* inform us that those given the service of the sanctuary carried this holy responsibility on their shoulders.

When I discovered all of this, about the importance of shoulders, I uncovered a deeper revelation of how God has placed us in a body that needs to function together to be effective. We're so used to taking more notice of the facial features, hands and feet that we often dismiss more vital parts that are essential for life,

> *"those parts of the body that seem to be
> weaker are indispensable."*
> 1 Corinthians 12:22 (NIV)

I became astutely aware that intercessors were vital in the work we were doing. We worked hard to bring the passion of Christ to life through open air theatre, but there were those who were working hard in the spirit realm, praying for God's will in all we were doing. Every person had a part to play. So too, do you. Each member within the body of Christ, needs to function accordingly. When you don't understand someone, it's imperative not to judge their behaviours and ways of thinking, just because it is alien to you. Different is not necessarily wrong. The way God has shown you, is not necessarily the best way, but it may be the right way for you. Let the light illuminate any dark areas in you, and permit the Holy Spirit to do His work in others.

If each individual focuses on their own walk with the Lord, His light can grow within them. Imagine then, how consequently, as that light shines brighter, its illumination will spill over to others. Thankfully, God doesn't need us to do His work for Him.

It is critical, we as the Church, recognise that we are not the same parts, but **part of the same body.**

> *"...there should be no division in the body,*
> *but that its parts should have equal concern*
> *for each other." 1 Corinthians 12:25 (NIV)*

God is calling us to work on a new found unity, like never before.

There will be a connecting of the body, and an arising of His bride. She will be radiant, pure, white, and dazzling; the world will have to take notice. You are His bride, His chosen. Hear his wooing and move in time with the rhythm of His heartbeat. Do not miss the bridegroom's call to the altar and so miss the wedding for you are His betrothed and it is time to get ready. Shift and change out of your old garment and into your wedding clothes.

In order to shine, she (the Bride of Christ) must first be cleansed. How does God clean and remove what is not of Him?

The following is another excerpt from the same word:

Many years ago, God spoke about a shaking. He said that He would shake the Church and then the world. The Church has been through a shaking, now the world.

Those being shaken have questioned, "Why?" "Where is God in this?" Many have been asking what they have done, as if it were a punishment that they were facing for some hidden sin. Too many have judged others, as with Job, believing the one being shaken was at blame for the suffering they have endured. Yes, God has been testing the heart, but He is a God of love and not condemnation. In His great wisdom, He had a plan. But to run the race, the athlete needs the strength and the stamina to endure. Only as the faith muscles are tested, are they ultimately strengthened.

Many in The Church have been on the edge of despair. They have felt as if they had no strength to endure. A bruised reed, He does not break, Isaiah 42:3. And countless warriors, who were at their weakest, experienced the depth of true faith. A faithful God will not break the covenant with those whom He has made a covenant with; those He has called and chosen. Even when we are unfaithful, God cannot be unfaithful to us.

> *"What if some were unfaithful? Will their unfaithfulness nullify God's faithfulness? Not at all! Let God be true, and every human being a liar."*
> *Romans 3:3-4. (NIV)*

The Church should discern the journey they have travelled. Like the Israelites who escaped the bondage of Egypt to enter an inheritance, it is time to shake off the slave mentality and give praise to the One who opens the door to promise.

The Holy Spirit alone is the one who imparts understanding enabling the eyes to see and to discern. To discern, is to see through the eyes of the Spirit and to know whose voice is speaking, whose hand is guiding.

Now is a time to praise, to give thanks, to worship in spirit and in truth –to the One who is worthy. God will have the Church shine, whilst the world looks on. For the world will be shaken. But God's people should not fear. They have been given an inoculation against the fear that will, and is come. Immunised through the testing of faith; strengthened through the trials. Trained for the season, equipped with heavenly armour, the Church should pray. Keeping eyes fixed above prayer will protect you; prayer will move mountains, break bondages, and pave the way for the miraculous. As the Church joins in unity through the bonds of the Spirit, the world will be in awe, as miracles take place. There will be counterfeit, but those who are called will come and will discern.

There is much that will take place, as the Word of God foretells, but even now the angels in Heaven are excited. They hear the rumble; they detect the times. They perceive the children of promise, returning home with their King.

If the Church walks in unity, it will shine, and the Holy Spirit will move in signs and wonders to the glory of God the Father, in the name of Jesus Christ.

> *"Strengthen the feeble hands, steady the knees that give way; say to those with fearful hearts, 'Be strong, do not fear; your God will come, he will*

*come with vengeance; with divine
retribution he will come to save you.'*

*Then will the eyes of the blind be
opened and the ears of the deaf
unstopped. Then will the lame leap
like a deer, and the mute tongue shout
for joy."*
Isaiah 35:3-6 (NIV)

I've mentioned some of the great heroes of our faith already and we'll be looking at Esther soon. But can you see the pattern?

Each one of these awesome characters who paved the way for us, were positioned. Joseph was positioned to save his family during the time of famine. Moses was then positioned to lead the children of Israel who'd grown in number, out of Egypt and to the promised land. Deborah was positioned as a judge over Israel and to see their enemy defeated. David was positioned to be the King of Israel in order to conquer their enemies and leave a legacy for generations to come. Esther, you will also read about, was positioned to save her people, the Jews. Can you see the pattern here? So often we get the focus wrong. It wasn't about them. Each one of them and many more throughout the Bible, were positioned not for themselves, but for others. They were sent ahead of time to rescue and save God's people.

You are being positioned, but it's not all about you.

JOURNAL YOUR THOUGHTS

BIBLE

PRAYER

17 ~

Chapter 17

PREPARATION

My husband and I laugh when we tell the story of how we married. We went from friends to newlywed in just three months. We skipped the *going-out* part, knowing that God had brought us together. I don't think many people who knew us both, thought it would last - but that was over thirty years ago.

Our journey hasn't been easy, but God knew what He was doing by joining us together so quickly. After my friend proposed to me (instead of asking me out whilst thinking, 'what have I done?!') and I replied 'yes' (whilst thinking, 'what about the going out part?'), there was a weightiness similar to what I described earlier. A heavy sense that God was deeply involved in our union. Although neither of us dreamt that we would be married so soon, we knew there was purpose in our relationship. Though not what we expected.

It possibly appeared to others that a rash momentary decision had been made. Yet, behind the scenes, God had been preparing each of us for that precise moment. For both of us that preparation looked different. I'd recently left the ministry team I was part of to move back to my hometown. That year was painful. I felt as if I'd been ripped away from my family and the deep sense of loss took time to heal. Little did I know that this was the start of the process God was taking me through in preparation for marriage.

Several months later, I woke up with a strong awareness of two things. Firstly, that I was about to start a new life, and secondly I was given a date - September. Since I'd been invited to join a touring dance company in the United States, I assumed this is what God was indicating to me. He told me to give away my car and many other belongings in preparation. I did so in obedience, in expectation of a September move. That isn't quite the whole story, but in order to condense it for this purpose, just know that the Holy Spirit was at work preparing my heart too. He was also preparing my husband in ways unbeknown to me, since he was living halfway across the country at the time.

In fact, there were many little miracles and signs along the way that we now enjoy reminiscing about because it was so evident God was in the details and the timing!

Cutting a very long and quite humorous story short, I can tell you that we were married in September that year. The day before our wedding, my husband was accepted into bible college (he applied after we'd set the wedding date). Following a two week honeymoon we went straight from the airport to the college, arriving on the first day of term. See what I mean about **God's timing**? We couldn't have planned it any better. God had us right where He wanted us.

In the book of *Esther, chapter 2* you can read about Esther's bridal preparations. She underwent twelve months of beauty treatment, before marrying King Xerxes. An entire year of spa-like pampering and preparation, wow!

Esther was an orphan, raised by her uncle Mordecai, but there was a call on her life and she rose to it. She was positioned to save the Jews from destruction and God caused her to find favour in the eyes of the King. As you read the story, you can see the strength within Esther. She was called to stand in the gap and present a petition to the King to spare the Jews who were about to be killed on his order. I believe God wasn't only preparing her body in the time of preparation. Whilst living in the palace, **He was preparing her in spirit**. Esther knew that she was putting her life at risk when she went into the inner court of the King without being summoned, (as her uncle had told her). But knowing that the lives of her people were at stake, gave her the ability to stand strong and say, *"if I perish, I perish."* *Esther 4:16*

When you look at the story more closely, you'll see that Esther didn't just blurt out her request. Surely, she breathed a huge sigh of relief when the King put out his sceptre, which meant she had found favour and wouldn't die (as his previous disrespectful wife had done). Most people would have seen that as a sign of God's favour and quickly put forward their plea. But Esther was much shrewder. She demonstrated a high level of grace in her actions, inviting the King and her enemy, Haman, to a banquet. She showed honour to her adversary who became pumped up with pride and was caught in his own trap.

Prior to this, Esther asked Mordecai to ask everyone to stand with her with prayer and fasting. During this time, it would seem God gave her the blueprint strategy to overcome their enemy. It's imperative to pause and listen before racing ahead when we think we've got a green light. Sometimes, there's a higher way filled with grace and mercy.

We know that God is preparing us, as His bride for the day of Jesus' return as the Bridegroom. The Bride (the Church) is to prepare herself. That includes you. It is time to get ready. This is your preparation. You may not know what is ahead. Just like Esther, the whole picture wasn't all mapped out clearly for her to see, but you can be confident that there is a plan. It is in this moment of preparation that we are strengthened, honed, graced, and lavished with love. Although it often isn't until you reflect on things afterwards that you can see what is happening. In my experience, God's love doesn't often appear all *lovey dovey*, pink and fluffy like some of the movies. It is strong and resilient, full of mercy and grace.

There is a place of residing, where the Father wants to lavish you with His love. To feel His heartbeat. To be at one with Him. I hear His whisper, like the bridegroom to his bride, wooing you to come. Come to Him and be in His presence. This is a time of the preparation of the heart.

> *"...because he loves me, I will rescue him.*
> *I will protect him, for he acknowledges My*
> *name."*
> *Psalm 91:14 (NIV)*

> *"Hallelujah! For our Lord God Almighty*
> *reigns. Let us rejoice and be glad and give*
> *him glory!*

For the wedding of the Lamb has come, and
his bride has made herself ready.
Fine linen, bright and clean, was given her
to wear."
Revelation 19: 6-8 (NIV)

Ultimately, Jesus gives us the model from which to live. He chose to lay His life down willingly of His own choice. In doing so, He knew the love of the Father was so strong that he would receive something back that was so much greater. Do you know the Father's love for you, in such a way, that you choose to willingly surrender your life for a greater good? I am not sure if anyone can truly answer that. I believe only the Holy Spirit can work this in you as He draws you deeper into the revelation of that love. For in all things, LOVE is the key; it is by very embodiment, God Himself.

"The reason my Father loves me is that I
lay down my life—only to take it up again.
No one takes it from me, but I lay it down
of my own accord. I have authority to lay
it down and authority to take it up again.
This command I received from my Father."
John 10:17-18 (NIV)

Jesus was prepared in His ministry to lay down His life, for you and me. We, too, are **being prepared**, as the Church, to give our lives for others. This may not mean literal death, but a death to self. Self-regard and ego. It is time to be accountable, be connected, be prepared. Ready for what lies ahead.

There is a spiritual battle being waged, and it will be won before the wedding of an **eternal lifetime.** There are forces seeking to abort this marriage, but it won't happen. Even now, there is an angelic presence being released. You don't need to focus on angels, but on Jesus. However, you can recognise their work, as you give glory to God. Recently, I sense not only an angelic army but also angelic worshippers and those who've gone before us to pave the way. It is as if they are all there, unseen, championing us on. Spurring you on to win the race and go for gold. A touch of Heaven coming down. On earth, as it is in Heaven.

Jeremiah is one of the most notable prophets in the Old Testament whom God used to warn the people to turn back to Him. The prophetic messages Jeremiah gave were often in contradiction to the *nice*, 'all will be wonderful' words given by the false prophets of the day. This led to him being persecuted and imprisoned. It was whilst Jeremiah was confined, being held prisoner, that God spoke to him. He was in his own lockdown, but the Lord reached out to him.

> *"This is what the Lord says, He who made the earth, the Lord who formed it and established it - the Lord is His name.* **Call to Me and I will answer you and tell you great and unsearchable things you do not know."**
> *Jeremiah 33:2-3 (NIV)*

Interestingly, God used lockdown across the globe to draw people closer to His heart. Many leaned into Him and began to hear some of these unsearchable things. This is a time like no other, where God wants to uncover secrets to His people. Those who yield themselves, will discover hidden treasures. That includes you.

> *"I will give you hidden treasures, riches*

stored in secret places, so that you may know
that I am the Lord, the God of Israel, who
summons you by name." Isaiah 45:3 (NIV)

Notice here that it isn't just to make you feel special. It is so that you will know it is the "God of Israel, who summons you by name."

Note also that if you struggle to comprehend any of what I've shared so far, be encouraged by what I'm about to share. God is no respecter of persons; even a child can receive wisdom from Heaven.

I've worked much of my life with young people from late teens and into their twenties. I love this age group who are often just finding themselves, and come with an insatiable thirst for understanding. A good debate in the classroom is a healthy way of helping young people to question and recognise where their beliefs come from. However, the danger can sometimes be that at a certain point those belief systems become rigid. Inflexible thinking can hinder a person from learning and adapting to new situations. Young children are generally the most teachable, as they aren't mature enough to know their own minds.

God calls us to come as these children, open to hearing from Him; to be teachable. As a teacher, I value education, but there is a place in God's classroom with teaching that excels beyond that of the natural realm. I invite you to come as a child, without preconceived ideas, into the throne room to receive an impartation from on high.

Be prepared to receive all that He longs to share with you.

"Jesus said, 'I praise you, Father, Lord of

*heaven and earth, because you have hidden
these things from the wise and learned, and
revealed them to little children.'"*
Matthew 11:25 (NIV)

The world is not just facing a physical war with ideological conflicts. It is a war that falls beyond the confines of the natural; we need spiritual eyes, for a spiritual battle. It's crucial that you truly know that you are being called by name and who it is that's calling you. No Government or human body of people has a solution to the global crises and onslaught of violence that our world is facing. They don't know how to fight a spiritual battle. It is time for the Church to arise from its internalisation and look upwards. It is time to see through new eyes, eyes of faith, eyes of the Spirit.

*"For we do not wrestle against flesh and
blood, but against principalities, against
powers, against the rulers of the darkness
of this age, against spiritual hosts of
wickedness in the heavenly places."*
Ephesians 6:12 (NKJV)

God is speaking to His Church, **"It is time to ARISE."**

Together, we can overcome the giants. We have the armour of God and weapons of warfare that will defeat even the most formidable foe.

Three of your greatest weapons are:

1. The Sword of the Spirit, knowing the Word of God and using it effectively. *Ephesians 6*

2. Unity with family in Christ - keeping the bond of peace. *"By this everyone will know that you are my disciples, if you love one another." John 13:35*

3. The weapon of worship...

My mother equipped me with one of the best weapons ever. She taught me to **praise** when things got tough. In the midst of trials, she would sing this song with me, "It's amazing what praising can do... Hallelujah, hallelujah".

What that did was teach me, no matter what circumstances I found myself in, I could lift my voice in praise to the One who was in control. I learnt how to worship in my innermost being, despite what I faced. Even when tears fell and pain gripped my soul, I chose to glorify the One who is above every other name. When you worship, whether through song, or word, or action, you are declaring God's lordship over your life and the situation. The enemy cannot stand in God's presence and when you worship, you are ushering His presence in. Where there is light, darkness has to flee.

It could be said that praise is an action, whereas worship is the condition of the heart. Praise is therefore an act of worship. When we worship, we make ourselves less, that He may be more. Whether laying prostrate, lifting your hands, kneeling or posturing before the Lord, it is the position of your heart that God sees.

*"Therefore I urge you, brothers and sisters, on account of God's mercy, to offer your bodies as living sacrifices, holy and pleasing to God, which is your **spiritual service of worship**. Do not be conformed to this*

*world, but be transformed by the renewing
of your mind. Then you will be able to test
and approve what is the good, pleasing, and
perfect will of God."*
Romans 12:1-2 (NIV)

This chapter is about preparation. Your **preparation** begins with your acts of **worship**.

In the scripture above, the description of offering your body as an act of spiritual worship precedes the all-important instruction in *verse 2*. The guidance here is to not be conformed to this world. This also means don't be fashioned to this world. Perhaps you can relate more to that? The fashions, trends and fads of this world are constantly changing. Sadly, too many people's lives revolve around them. There's nothing wrong with being fashionable, but adapting your life to accommodate worldly thinking as opposed to godly (biblical) thinking isn't going to yield fullness of life and quality fruit. God wants you to bear fruit that will last. The lusts of the flesh and worldly mindsets have us focussing on the wrong goal. When your mind is renewed by truth (Word based) thinking, your behaviours will also be transformed. Strengthen yourself in the Word of God and worship. Then you will be able to test and approve God's will. As it says, *"... the pleasing and perfect will of God."*

*"But the hour is coming, and is now here,
when the true worshipers will worship the
Father in spirit and truth, **for the Father
is seeking such people to worship
him**. God is spirit, and those who worship
him must **worship in spirit and
truth**." John 4:23-24 (ESV)*

It is in the midst of acts of worship that we are transformed.

You are changed when you **encounter God**. No-one can stay the same after being in His presence. As you offer yourself to Him at this time, note, this includes your whole body, not just your spirit. I believe God wants to release a greater freedom of expression through our worship with dance, music and various art forms. *2 Samuel 6* tells us that King David danced with all his might before the Lord in celebration of bringing the Ark of Lord back to the city. He did so amid shouting and trumpet playing. This was his act of worship. How do we know? Because firstly, they made sacrificial offerings along the journey, and secondly, David was wearing a linen ephod, which is a priestly garment. I've often heard sermons about him dancing in his underwear. This may be due to *verse 20* which talks about David uncovering himself. Some Bible versions say half-naked. The original Hebrew word used here is *galah*, which means uncover, discover, reveal, open, show, remove, appear. Whether or not the verse infers that David was in his underwear, I believe that the uncovering is not so much about his clothing (since the priest traditionally wore ephods), but more about his willingness to be *undignified* before the Lord.

> *"...Therefore I will play music before the Lord. And I will be even more undignified than this, and will be humble in my own sight."*
> 2 Samuel 6:21-22 (*NKJV*)

David **exposed his heart.** He was willing to reveal his inner self. He demonstrated his worship for God openly expressing his emotions without concern about what others thought. This is a challenge to us all.

The Bible also tells us that battles can be won through **praise and worship**. The battle of Jericho was won when the walls came down, after the Israelites marched around the city for seven days as the trumpeters played. Joshua 6. Jehoshaphat was given victory after sending out singers to praise the Lord.

> *"Jehoshaphat appointed men to sing to the Lord and to praise him for the splendor of his holiness as they went out at the head of the army, saying: "Give thanks to the Lord, for his love endures forever." As they began to sing and praise, the Lord set ambushes against the men of Ammon and Moab and Mount Seir who were invading Judah, and they were defeated."*
> *2 Chronicles 20:21-22 (NIV)*

It isn't just about singing or playing instruments, it is about a heart position. God wants you to align with a new victory mindset using the weapon of worship. What better example of this is there, than when the apostles, Paul and Silas were locked up in prison? Despite their situation, they chose to focus on the One who is able. They worshipped amid their imprisonment.

> *"But at midnight Paul and Silas were praying and **singing hymns to God**, and the prisoners were listening to them. Suddenly there was a great earthquake, so that the foundations of the prison were shaken; and immediately all the doors were opened and everyone's **chains were loosed**."*
> *Acts 16:25-26*

It is also important to note that you cannot twist God's arm. Praise and worship is not a magic trick to change a situation you don't like. It is about **aligning with God's will**. Praying not my will, by thine Lord. *Luke 22:42* As you are being prepared for the next season, you can learn a fundamental lesson from Habakkuk. Habakkuk was a lesser-known prophet who heard directly from the Lord. God revealed to him that, after a time of discipline, He would restore Israel. Habakkuk saw in the spirit a time of blessing and restoration. However, it didn't happen in his lifetime. Yet, Habakkuk chose to rejoice in spite of not seeing what had been promised. He believed God and trusted in His faithfulness.

> *"Though the fig tree does not bud and there are no grapes on the vines, though the olive crop fails and the fields produce no food, though there are no sheep in the pen and no cattle in the stalls, yet I will rejoice in the Lord, I will be joyful in God my Savior."*
> *Habakkuk 3:17-18 (NIV)*

If I'd known in advance the journey my husband and I would have to face, with all the trials we've gone through over the years, I'd probably have run a mile in the opposite direction. Yet today, I am grateful for the course I've had to take, because it has made me who I am. When an oyster is presented with a parasite or irritant, I'm sure it doesn't get excited and say, 'yippee'. But it is forced to use its defence system, secreting a substance that creates a mother of pearl material. The formation of the valued pearl that Jesus compares to the Kingdom of Heaven, in terms of worth *Matthew 13:45-46*, is made out of an aggravation - something unwanted. Whatever your journey, can you **discern the preparation**?

JOURNAL YOUR THOUGHTS

BIBLE

PRAYER

18 ~

Chapter 18

SIGN OF THE TIMES

Semiotics is the study of signs and one of my favourite teaching topics. To recognise the sign of the times we are living in, helps if you have a greater understanding of semiotics. You are surrounded by signs that seek to direct your attention daily. Every moving or still image or sound is a **signifier,** i.e. a sign that communicates some type of message to you. These signifiers come in all types of forms. Whether it is a photograph, a piece of text, a physical object, or sound of any kind, you are surrounded by these signifiers. In fact, even the way an image or video is presented is a signifier; as it encodes a meaning.

I won't go into too much more detail here, but you will already be familiar with how they can impact behaviour. For example, you could wake up and hear water tapping at your window, or see a sky full of dark clouds. These signs signify to you that it is raining, or is likely to rain. Therefore, you may choose to grab an umbrella. Next you jump into your car, only to notice that the needle is on red, signifying that you need to fill up with fuel. You set off for the garage, but there is a big red circle with a white line through it, signifying no entry. Adjacent to it an arrow signifies to you that you should follow it, in order to get to your desired destination.

Each of those signs are learnt. The no entry sign is a universally recognised signifier and many other road signs you probably learnt about if you studied the highway code. However, learning about the weather didn't need much studying. Experience of getting wet was probably enough. Seeing flashes of lightning across the sky pre-empting loud thunder crashes are signifiers of an oncoming storm. We'll look at how Jesus talks about these signs in a moment. But you'll recognise that these signifiers are actually visual and audio clues to what weather we can expect.

Every day, you are bombarded with signifiers through the media. Whether you're watching a film, TV, YouTube, or something on social media, listening to the radio or streaming service, or whatever content you like to consume, you'll engage with signifiers. Your brain processes hundreds of these signifiers every day. They are like numerous pieces of coded information that you interpret in nanoseconds. However, there are a few key things you should be aware of. In the first instance, the signifiers embedded in media are intentional; you are constantly being 'sold' something. It could be a product, service, an opinion, concept or idea. Advertising is both blatant and subtle. Not all advertising is negative, it is just a way of informing others of what is being offered. Churches, for example, use marketing to promote their services and events. Although, even church promotion can be both good and bad. Think about the Church promotions you see. Does it appeal to people, as the place to help them find solutions to their daily challenges, and lead them effectively to God? Does it say, we stand for righteousness and justice; we will protect and support you - be there for you, so you're not walking alone? Does it promote a place of strength and dignity? Hmm, a little food for thought there.

Most people are aware that brands are selling to them, but you probably won't notice some of the more covert messaging that is planted. For example, everyone is familiar with the famous Amazon brand logo, but did you notice the smiling mouth of the yellow arrow pointing from A to Z in its name? This doesn't have any negative connotations, as its message suggests that it provides and delivers everything you could want from A to Z. But, it demonstrates how subtle some messaging can be.

Sexual connotations are implied regularly in advertising, as it is well known that sex sells. We've perhaps become too accustomed to it. The monetisation of sexualised content is prolific, embedded in adverts for fragrance, alcohol, clothing, and pretty much everything else. The use of images, sounds, colour, style, positioning of people and objects are all intrinsically encoded to entice you, or provoke you, in some way or another. Signifiers embedded in media aim to promote an emotive response. That, in turn, drives behaviour. Consider how particular images, for example, food or drink, affect how you feel. In a simplistic form, you see an ad for something that stirs a positive emotion, so you now associate that product with a particular feeling. You are then more likely to reach for that *feeling* - in the same way a social media *like* provides a dopamine hit, giving you a *feel-good* moment.

However, this has impacted negatively on the mental wellbeing of so many young people, in particular. Almost everything you see or hear is promoting an agenda. Sadly, too many people are oblivious to the undercover techniques that are used in attempting to influence them. Many seek to alter or impact behaviours and beliefs. In a world of fake news and misinformation, it is challenging to discern what is real. The reality is even mainstream news have published fake news, albeit possibly not having verified their own journalism. Have you unknowingly forwarded misinformation (whether verbally or through social media)? Would you even know if you've been fed fake news? This topic isn't something to be afraid of or shy away from. It is something that you should be seeking to understand, so that you can discern what you are consuming and discern the motive behind it.

It is reassuring to remember that throughout time, imitations have been made. Consider the golden calf and other false idols that sought to distract God's people's attention away from the One True God. We need not fear, but we do need to discern. God is teaching His people how to **discern truth from deception.** The Holy Spirit is at work providing His own signifiers for us to see and hear and take note of. The key is learning to identify them.

It is important to put this into **Biblical context**. Several chapters ago, we explored what God is speaking about a crossroads and our need for signposts. The sign literally posts you in the right direction.

So, what does the Bible say about signs?

Observing the Old Testament in relation to the New Testament unpacks much revelation. It warns, informs, and encourages us. In order to understand and discern the times, we look for signs. This is exactly what the Pharisees did. They demanded a sign from Jesus, who identified their lack of ability to interpret the signs of the times. He told them that they had already been given the sign - of Jonah. (You can read the book of Jonah to learn more). But here you can note that the Pharisees understood how to read the signs through nature when looking at the sky, but they were unable to interpret the signs of the times, because their hearts were not open.

> *"The Pharisees and Sadducees came to Jesus and tested him by asking him to* **show them a sign** *from heaven." "He (Jesus) replied, "When evening comes, you say, 'It will be fair weather, for the sky is red,' and in the morning, 'Today it will be stormy, for the sky is red and overcast.' You know how to interpret the appearance of the sky, but you cannot* **interpret the signs of the times**. *A wicked and adulterous generation looks for a sign, but none will be given it except the sign of Jonah." "*
> *Matthew 16: 1-4 (NIV)*

This is a good place to pause and reflect on **how you interpret the times** we're living in. I see many people fathoming things through the natural lens in conjunction with politics, inflation, house prices, energy costs, technological developments, social media, fashion, trends... and so forth. It's time to evaluate how you process. What impacts on how you think and consequently behave? Consciously listen to what you say, it will **open your ears in a new way.** How much of what you speak out loud, aligns with the Word of God?

Every word is conceived in your unconscious mind. Not just your thoughts (though this is a good place to start), but deep inside your being. Your mind is not just your brain, but a connection to your heart. Neither is this just in a physiological way. It has a deep connection to your inner gut. It all begins in your spirit, stemming from your belief system. If this is built upon the rock *(i.e. Jesus Christ, the Word of God)*, then in times of instability, you will stand. "For no one can lay any foundation other than the one already laid, which is Jesus Christ." *Matthew 7:24-27*. All else is sand, so it's imperative to know where your belief system is founded.

Let's double back to the remark Jesus made about the sign of Jonah. This is in reference to His resurrection after 3 days of burial. We can see that Jesus was speaking about a prophetic sign. This highlights why **you need spiritual eyes and ears to discern what God is speaking.**

The story of Jonah also carries another relevant message for us today.

Jonah did not run from God because he was afraid to preach to the Ninevites. Jonah disobeyed God's call to go to Nineveh, because he was angry with God. Jonah was an Israelite and Nineveh was an Assyrian city full of non-Jewish Gentiles. The Ninevites were behaving wickedly, but they did so in ignorance. They didn't know any better! Jonah knew that if he went and helped to open their eyes to the evil they were doing that they would repent and God would forgive them. Jonah knew the heart of God. And he didn't want them to be forgiven; he didn't want mercy to be extended to them. Look at their response to Jonah's message.

> *"... Let everyone call urgently on God.*

*Let them give up their evil ways and their
violence. Who knows? God may yet relent
and with compassion turn from his fierce
anger so that we will not perish."
Jonah 3:8-9 (NIV)*

The people of Nineveh called out to God and He
demonstrated His grace and compassion. What an
amazing moment in history. An entire non-Jewish Gentile
nation turned away from their sins to acknowledge the One
True God.

Around 800 years later, Simon Peter came to the same
realisation. God called him to lead a centurion named
Cornelius and his family to Christ. Cornelius wasn't a Jew,
but a righteous man respected by the Jews. Peter had a
dream where he heard a voice telling him,

*"Do not call anything impure that God has
made clean." Acts 10: 15 (NIV)*

The dream was with regards to food, in as much that Jews
were not supposed to eat certain kinds of unclean animals,
and it was revealed to Peter that all things are made clean
and all meat could be eaten. Nevertheless, the message
being sent through the dream was not so much about food,
but about salvation. Initially, it was assumed that Jesus was
only the King of the Jews. The belief was that salvation was
for the Jewish community only, but if you continue studying
chapter 10, you'll see Peter is given a revelation of how God
came to save all people. Cornelius and his family were saved
because Peter allowed his eyes to be opened to accepting
that Jesus died on the cross for both Jew and Gentile. What
Peter had previously deemed unclean, God accepted. Peter

learnt more about God's grace and love. **The Creator's heart for all of His creation**. It is God alone who saves.

When Jonah finally repented himself, for his own disobedience, he acknowledged this profound statement, "Salvation comes from the Lord."

> *"But I, with shouts of grateful praise,*
> *will sacrifice to you. What I have vowed*
> *I will make good. I will say, 'Salvation*
> *comes from the Lord.'"*
> *Jonah 2:9 (NIV)*

Pause and let the Holy Spirit illuminate that awesome truth afresh to your spirit.

As you read on in *Jonah 4*, you will see that he quickly forgot the words he'd spoken after the Ninevites repented, and he went outside the city to sulk. Jonah was angry with God for relenting and showing mercy to an ungodly people. Surely, this is a challenge to our own hearts. It is not easy to walk in love and compassion towards those who demonstrate a lifestyle of behaviours like that of the Ninevites. If nothing else, this should be a wake-up call to recognise that God is speaking through His word to our hearts; provoking us to positive action. God didn't allow the Ninevites to continue in their godless ways, but He removed their blind sightedness in order for them to receive His loving grace and forgiveness.

How do you begin to love when you see so much that is contrary to what you know or believe God stands for? When you're faced with seemingly mixed messages, how do you find the truth? Jesus, when faced with temptation during his extreme wilderness experience, was combated by the devil with the Word. The enemy can appear as an angel of light quoting scriptures and performing wonders in an attempt to deceive, as the Bible says, *"...if possible, even the elect." Matthew 24:24*

We are in a time where **what you think you know, will be shaken.**

Recently, I attended a networking event where the compere asked us a series of ice-breaking, *getting to know you* questions. Let me take a moment here to ask you a few similar questions:

1. Do you put cereal in the bowl first or the milk?
2. On holiday do you prefer to sunbathe by the pool all day or explore?
3. French fries or chipshop chips? - with gravy or ketchup?

Now we all know the answers. Certainly, you have to put the cereal in the bowl before the milk because then you know how much to pour. I can hear a round of yeses. But maybe a few resolute nos? I was shocked how many people actually put the milk in first! I could continue through the list of questions, and no doubt it would stir up more intense feelings. Until this point at the networking event, the guests had gathered in polite conversation with drinks in hand. But now the drinks were down, voices were raised, and hands were waving all over the place. There was some strong opposition in the room. A series of simple questions had brought a new energy to the meeting space. Although, all in good jest, we became highly opinionated with our own ways of doing things. I was fascinated at my own and others' emotive responses. When those people on either side of me agreed, we felt our solidarity growing. Simultaneously, division grew in opposition to those who had alternative views. You could see more of an *us* and *them* taking place. It was actually a fun way of getting to know one another. Nobody took it seriously, but it is a great example of how we can become entrenched in strong opinions that, at the end of the day, are irrelevant in the bigger scheme of things.

Some of our inherent ideologies and belief systems have been built on man-made systems that are **being shaken**.

Many doctrines of belief stem from tradition. Tradition in itself is not bad. It often begins with a well-meaning practice. The repetition of this may then become a regular custom or ceremony. Most families have their own traditions that they've built up over years. Those traditions or rituals are not necessarily negative. It could be said that it is a **culture** that has been produced and nurtured over time within a people group. However, when we become so accustomed to a traditional or cultural way of doing something, without question, there's the potential for becoming dogmatic. There's a temptation to think that if something works, then it is the best or right way of doing things, expecting others to agree or take up your beliefs. This form of tradition or dogma can result in a pious religiosity that isn't born out of love and acceptance. The result of this bears potential for pride and arrogance.

Do you question where certain philosophies or principles originate from? What rationales do you use to explain your thoughts or behaviours? Has the outcome strayed from its original intent? What I mean by this is, where do your foundational beliefs stem from?

Remember what I explained about semiotics, and the signs you've learnt to interpret. It's worth noting at this point that many of the signifiers you identify are also culturally learnt. Your upbringing, education, background, social standing, ethnicity, the place you live and more... all impact on how you make sense of the world and how you interpret the signs around you. Whether you put cereal or milk in your bowl first, is likely to have stemmed from your upbringing. Not only your family, but your peers would have had a big influence on your beliefs and behaviours.

The word cow, for most of us, will provoke images of farms, countryside, milk, or meat, and a famous burger joint, for obvious reasons. Or possibly a well-known nursery rhyme that you were taught alongside images of cows in a children's nursery book. However, in certain countries a cow is treated as sacred, or seen as a sign of wealth. A bit like my Tunisian friend earlier, with his camels!

One word or image consequently creating differing responses. The word *orange* is another polysemic signifier, meaning it has more than one possible interpretation. You may think it means the colour or alternatively the fruit. Only **in context** does it truly make the fullest sense. So, as you watch and listen for the signs God is giving you, recognize both your inherent bias (based on your own limited understanding - we are all foolish in comparison to God), and ensure you put them into context. Taking a single sign and making it say what you want, is not wisdom.

So what are the **signs of the time**?

Can you see and hear what the Spirit is doing in our time?

In acknowledging that our foundation is the Bible - the Word of God, we must also keep our hearts soft to the leading of the Spirit. To allow Him to cast light in any areas of misinformation or deception. This is not to fear being deceived, but to trust in the God of love to reveal His life, in all its fullness. The Bible makes it very clear that sin is what separates us from God and His grace is not a licence to sin. However, Jesus took the punishment for all sin upon Himself at the cross, and gave Himself up for all sinners.

> "...*There is no difference between Jew and Gentile, for **all have sinned and fall short of the glory of God**, and all are justified freely by his grace through the redemption that came by Christ Jesus. God presented Christ as a sacrifice of atonement, through the shedding of his blood—to be received by faith.*"
> *Romans 3:22-26 (NIV)*

God, in His love, is reaching out to you to **help you discern.** He is speaking to His Church and showing you the **signs**. He is about to move in a magnificent way and the Holy Spirit is looking to equip, train and prepare you for what He's about to do. So that you are positioned for purpose.

Psalm 119 is full of encouragement for you to find your anchor in the Word. As you meditate on it, allow that still small voice to speak to you. "Seek and you will find", *Matthew 7:7*

JOURNAL YOUR THOUGHTS

BIBLE

PRAYER

Can You Hear the Call to
be Positioned for Purpose?

19 ~

Chapter 19

HE WHO HAS EARS

Braindead is an American TV show that was broadcast in 2016. It is a political satire and comic sci-fi show. The story revolves around extremely polarised political parties in the US government. Each opponent in the war of politics is obstinate and unmoving in their stance, as they battle it out against each other. The irony of this is that the politics is not the main drama playing out, and is in fact a distraction to the real plot. The politicians are oblivious in their conflicts that there is something else more sinister playing out before them.

The real situation is that a meteor has crashed to earth containing brain eating bugs that want to take over the world. These alien ants crawl inside politicians' heads via their ears, making them behave bizarrely. The tiny insignificant ants cause the characters to focus on their differences, whilst they secretly begin to dominate the human race. Right under their noses, in fact, but they are too blind to see what is really happening.

This absurd show is a powerful example of how the enemy can use trifling issues to distract your attention from matters of true importance. When God's people are unable to unite because of matters that don't impact on our eternal inheritance, one has to question. It comes back to the affairs **of the heart**. When you are unsure of your own motives, you can test to see how much of the Holy Spirit is flowing through you, by the evidence of the fruit of the Spirit in our life: love, joy, peace, forbearance, kindness, goodness, faithfulness, gentleness and self-control. *Galatians 5:22-23.*

You will find revelation of these things in the place of stillness.

On a side note, let me share a moment of revelation I received that you may find helpful. I used to feel as if I was a constant failure. I was unable to walk in all of the fruits of the Spirit, no matter how much I strived to do so. Just like the wretchedness that Paul describes in *Romans 7*, we do not do what we want to do because of our flesh. Yet, in that moment of revelation, I understood. It is not something that we try and do, but rather it is WHO HE IS! The great **I Am** within us. It is He that outworks this in us, as we continue to yield ourselves to Him - the One *who is* Love - *who is* Joy - *who is* Peace, and so forth... It is not so much that we live with the Spirit in doing all these things. Rather, it is the Spirit who expresses Himself through us, by these fruits, as we are yielded to Him.

You will receive even greater revelation as you **listen**.

Sitting in my great granny and grandad's house as a child felt like an eternity. There was little to do, but a whole space of nothing. Nothing that is, except the clocks. I'm not sure how many clocks there were, but I'm convinced the one on the mantelpiece in the sitting room had the loudest tick ever. Tick, tock, tick, tock... The sound would echo around my head sending me into a comatose state (or so I felt as a child), as I waited for the time to go by. Then, at the top of the hour, a moment of excitement took place. I'd be mesmerised for free seconds, as a tiny door in the clock on the wall would open, and out would emerge a little cuckoo bird. I'd listen to it telling me the time "cuckoo, cuckoo", before it disappeared for another hour. Simultaneously, the big grandad clock in the hallway would chime a deep sound that echoed through the house.

Sometimes, it isn't until time has passed and there's space to reflect, that we understand. In those days, time seemed to pass slowly. I felt bored on many occasions. But as I look back, I see through a different lens. What appeared to be empty, was in fact full of treasure. However, I was too young to understand the value of that emptiness. I could not have comprehended how rich a place to pause can be. In the seeming silence, I heard those things that you don't notice at first. The sound of birds singing, distant traffic noise, the clicking of knitting needles, my great grandad's gentle breathing. There is so much sound we take for granted.

My grandma's house was also very quiet, but she taught me another rich lesson. Since she couldn't drive, we would walk everywhere. No matter where we went, she would stop every so often and point something out to me. "Oh, look," she would say. I'd look and there she'd point, "a little robin redbreast, shh... keep very still." So, we'd stand and watch very quietly. Eventually, we'd move on, but again there would be a squirrel and I'd hear her say, "Look he's burying his nuts for the winter. I wonder how many that little fella has under there? I expect he's hidden them in different places, so the other squirrels won't find them."

I didn't appreciate these moments until I was much older and my grandma would look after my own children. She taught each of us a valuable experience. She taught us how to listen, as well as to see. To stop, to pause, to take time and observe. To notice what others missed.

In the place of stillness, when you quieten your soul before Him, you will hear.

A space created without rush, just a moment of hush, opens a treasure trove. Note, the hearing isn't always immediate. When God has spoken to me, I don't always receive the message straight away. It may be in the middle of night that the insight and hearing comes. At other times it is on hindsight that I can see clearly what He has whispered in the stillness. This leads me back to the story I began much earlier...

I told you I'd tell you more about how I made King Carl and Queen Sylvia of Sweden chuckle. Well, the entire audience was in full-blown laughter as I was in full flow, sharing the Gospel through the story of Jonah. But at one point, I emphasised my own position. Little did I realise what I had done and the embarrassment I had just brought upon the compere who was translating for me. Unbeknown to me, this man was a national Swedish celebrity and a devout atheist. Not only had he found himself in a situation where I was talking about the stubbornness of Jonah who rebelled when God spoke, but I'd also got him to proclaim, "I believe, Jesus is Lord."

Only years later did I recognise the revelation that this was what God had already spoken to me about (the details are for my ears alone).

Yet the word declares that every tongue will confess that Jesus is Lord, *Philippians 2:11*.

The point here is that God is at work and will move in ways we cannot fathom, but if you are prepared, you will hear things with your spiritual ears and then see them outwork before your eyes. We are in a time unlike any other. We shift towards and are in a new dispensation. You need new eyes and new ears to see and hear the new. Are you prepared to let go of the old ways, to see and hear afresh what the Lord is speaking?

It appears the more I learn about God and His ways, the less I know.

Are you willing to let go of what you thought you knew? Are you prepared to be wrong?

> *"Do not deceive yourselves. If any of you think you are wise by the standards of this age, you should become "fools" so that you may become wise. For the wisdom of this world is foolishness in God's sight."*
> *1 Corinthians 3: 18-19 (NIV)*

The Bible continues in the subsequent verses, to illuminate how even the boast in human leaders is foolish. The chapter pinpoints how division arose amongst the Church, as they each sought to follow different leaders. It is a stark reminder that our boast must be in the Lord. If you lift up human beings to prefer one over another, there will be disagreements.

At the same time, you should recognise that leaders are established by God, *Romans 13*. That is not a new concept, but it's important to discern and recognise that God even raises up oppressive leaders, as we note in *Exodus 9:16*, where Pharaoh is raised up, for the display of God's splendour. Why? So that God's name would be proclaimed throughout the earth. The book of *Habakkuk* reinforces this. God raised up the Chaldeans to discipline the children of Israel to learn an important lesson. As mentioned previously, Habakkuk didn't see the promise fulfilled, but still he stood by faith on what God had revealed to him. In discerning the times, we need to remember that it is **by faith**, with eyes of faith and ears of faith, and it is always for His Glory.

However, discerning is not always easy (as noted previously). Even bible heroes faced these dichotomies, like Simon Peter, when confronted with his preconceived ideas. So, I asked the Lord, where should we start to stand on the Word and walk in wisdom? This is where I was led, to Proverbs, which gives us an anchor from which we can stand.

> *"The fear of the Lord is the beginning of wisdom, and knowledge of the Holy One is understanding."*
> *Proverbs 9: 10 (NIV)*

If our hearts are pliable to God, open to being wrong, yet held by a holy, reverent fear - a depth of profound respect that stems from our love for Our Saviour, then we will have found our anchor. In His arms, we find truth. In that secret place, alone with our God, we learn about who He is, the Alpha and Omega, the first and the last, the beginning and the end *Revelations 22:13*

A surety comes from knowing, He alone is GOD, Our Creator. We can trust in His authority, guidance, and faithfulness to the covenant of love that He has made with us, as His creation. We may fall short at times and see only in part, but as our hearts are yielded in this way, by faith, with Jesus on the throne of our lives, the Holy Spirit will direct us.

In this way, it is possible to let go of misconceptions and preconceived ideas about others. God calls you to honour one another. There has been a culture of disrespect and disdain towards others that is not in alignment with the call to rise above. To discern is to understand the heart of God and recognise His hand at work. We are all made in His image, in His likeness and He calls you to submit yourself, as a servant in serving a higher purpose. It is embodied in love. That is *who* you are serving, Love Himself, by loving and honouring others. Throughout the Word of God, we are exhorted to honour. To prefer others, and treat them with respect. Please note sin is not honoured. An ungodly lifestyle is not honoured, but the call is to rise above vengeful or selfish ways; seek to honour God by preferring others above yourself, and treating them with dignity.

One translation is interpreted as, **'outdo one another in showing honour.'** *Romans 12:10 ESV.* That is surely a gauntlet being thrown out to spur us on to greater love.

Is this easy? By no means! But it can be your goal, your desire, the ethos by which you seek to live. Beyond this, there is another mandate to those whom God has raised as faithful spiritual leaders in authority.

> *"The elders who direct the affairs of the Church well are worthy of **double honour,** especially those whose work is preaching and teaching."* *1 Timothy 5:17.*

243

How do you honour those God has raised in authority within the Church?

Do you notice their every imperfections, or the call and anointing on their life? Let us not forget the log in our own eye, *Matthew 7: 3-5*. In honouring, you align with He who is Love.

I believe that God is identifying a moment of rapture. A juncture where we are being given the opportunity to be drawn into a death-defying love. To be caught up with the One who is love. Your Saviour is calling you into His embrace, to be raptured in His presence. Encompassed, you will hear the sound of His heartbeat, and yours will harmonise with its rhythm.

It is time to be aligned to His heart.

When you walk down the street or scroll through social media, do you hear the cries of those still in bondage and slavery, seeking a Messiah to release them from their captivity? What do you hear? Can you hear the love your Saviour has for you? Can you hear the whispers of the One who breathed life into every person on earth? Do you hear His heart that yearns for His creation to find healing and wholeness?

> *"The Spirit of the Sovereign Lord is on me, because the Lord has anointed me to proclaim good news to the poor. He has sent me to bind up the brokenhearted, to proclaim freedom for the captives and release from darkness for the prisoners, to proclaim the year of the Lord's favor and the day of vengeance of our God, to comfort all who*

*mourn, and provide for those who grieve
in Zion— to bestow on them a crown of
beauty instead of ashes, the oil of joy
instead of mourning, and a garment of
praise instead of a spirit of despair..."*
Isaiah 61: 1-3 (NIV)

This is a well-known Scripture, relevant as ever for this time. But notice the language here. The pronoun used is 'me' referring to the One who was reading the scripture in *Luke 4:21* when Jesus said, *"Today this scripture is fulfilled in your hearing."* I find this encouraging because it means it is He, the Great I Am, who brings the healing and does the liberating. That takes any unhealthy burden or yoke from our shoulders and puts it firmly on Jesus. However, in the following verses, it changes to 'they', meaning us, the body of Christ who will rebuild the ruined cities. It is **Jesus by the Holy Spirit in you** *(and I)* who opens blind eyes, and gives birth physical and spiritual sight. He is the worker of wonders and miracles, He alone saves. But we are called to bring the restoration where there has been devastation. Are you ready to build? The fields are indeed white for harvest. Will you join the labourers? *Luke 10:2*

*"...They will be called oaks of
righteousness, a planting of the Lord for the
display of his splendor. They will rebuild
the ancient ruins and restore the places long
devastated; they will renew the ruined cities
that have been devastated for generations."*
Isaiah 61: 3-4 (NIV)

I believe we are living on the brink of something unprecedented - this new dispensation - **an explosion of grace**. A time we would never have believed had someone told us before. What we are entering is a space that God alone wants to fill.

There is a calling, a wooing of the Spirit, drawing the Church into the arms of the bridegroom. As a woman that analogy is possibly easier to relate to. Yet the disciple John provides a great example of this. Throughout the Book of *John*, which he authored, John describes himself as the disciple Jesus loved. In *chapter 13* he recounts the Last Supper. Unlike the other Gospel accounts, John identifies himself in this way, as leaning on Jesus. The KJV provides a more intimate (non-sexual) description.

> *"Now there was leaning on Jesus' bosom,*
> *one of his disciples, whom Jesus loved."*
> *John 13:23.*

This close proximity of John to Jesus means he quite possibly heard **Jesus' heartbeat**. It perhaps indicates a greater awareness of the disciple to the heart of Jesus. This is most likely why John's Gospel is full of revelation. Unlike the other three Gospels, John is the only writer who actually knew Jesus personally. He writes his account from personal experience, which makes it stand out differently from the others. John's version of events reveals the person of Jesus, as the Christ, the divinity of God. This is the revelation given by the disciple who knew he was loved, and who loved in return.

God wants you to know how **loved** you are. There is a calling to return back to the first love. This is the place where the things of this world pale into insignificance. The things of everlasting value transcend all earthly treasure. A positioning where you feel the very heartbeat of God. The place where He reveals and entrusts those who love Him with intimate secrets. Your ears will hear beyond this realm. God wants to share with you.

> *"Call to me and I will answer you and tell you great and unsearchable things you do not know."*
> *Jeremiah 33:3*

> *"My message and my preaching were not with wise and persuasive words, but with a demonstration of the Spirit's power, so that your **faith might not rest on human wisdom, but on God's power**."*
> *1 Corinthians 2:4-5 (NIV)*

In seeking to live in accordance with His Will and His heart, God will, by His Spirit, help you to **discern the time** that we are living in. You have been equipped with the Sword of the Spirit, which is the Word of God, your Bible.

> *"For the word of God is alive and active. Sharper than any double-edged sword, it penetrates even to dividing soul and spirit, joints and marrow; it judges the thoughts and attitudes of the heart."*
> *Hebrews 4:12 (NIV)*

In summing up how we should live, *Romans 12* gives us a beautiful outline to offer our bodies, be a living sacrifice, holy and pleasing to God, walking humbly without judgement, in the gifts He has bestowed on us, demonstrating love in action. I encourage you to go and meditate on the entire chapter.

> *"And this is my prayer: that your love may*
> *abound more and more in knowledge and*
> *depth of insight, so that you may be able to*
> *discern what is best and may be pure and*
> *blameless for the day of Christ, filled with*
> *the fruit of righteousness that comes through*
> *Jesus Christ — to the glory and praise*
> *of God."*
> *Philippians 1:9-11 (NIV)*

In conclusion, I began in the introduction with *Romans 13: 11*, and I will also finish with it. But given here in a fuller context with the verses that precede it.

> *"Let no debt remain outstanding, except*
> *the continuing debt to love one another, for*
> *whoever loves others has fulfilled the law.*
> *The commandments, "You shall not commit*
> *adultery," "You shall not murder," "You*
> *shall not steal," "You shall not covet,"and*
> *whatever other command there may be, are*
> *summed up in this one command: "Love*
> *your neighbour as yourself." Love does no*
> *harm to a neighbour. Therefore love is the*
> *fulfilment of the law."*
> *"And do this,* **understanding the**
> **present time.."**
> *Romans 13: 8-11 (NIV)*

JOURNAL YOUR THOUGHTS

BIBLE

PRAYER

NOT THE END...

THIS IS JUST THE BEGINNING!

ENDNOTES

Additional References and Further Reading:

Pg 81, *Eye* Pg 50, *Chronos.* Pg 51, *Moed.* Pg 52, *Kairos. Pg 215 Galah* - Strong, J., 1996. New Strong's exhaustive concordance. Nashville: Nelson Reference & Electronic, a division of Thomas Nelson Publishers.

Pg 39, *Dispensation* Pg 43, *Sanctum* - Dictionary.com. 2022. Dictionary.com | Meanings and Definitions of Words at Dictionary.com. [ONLINE] Available at: https://www.dictionary.com. [Accessed 15 December 2022]

Pg 85,*Sulatna Disaster* - Sultana Museum. 2022. The Sultana Disaster. [ONLINE] Available at: https://www.thesultanaassociation.com. [Accessed 15 December 2022]
Wikipedia. 2022. The Sultana Steamboat. [ONLINE] Available at: https://en.wikipedia.org/wiki/Sultana_(steamboat). [Accessed 15 December 2022]

Pg 95, *Old ship use* - Ship-technology.com. 2022. New Uses for Old Cruise Ships. [ONLINE] Available at: https://www.ship-technology.com/analysis/profiling-world-most-bizarre-uses-old-cruise-ships/. [Accessed 15 December 2022]
Maritime-executive.com. 2022. Two Cruise Ships Join New Orleans Hurricane Relief Efforts. [ONLINE] Available at: https://maritime-executive.com/article/two-cruise-ships-join-new-orleans-hurricane-relief-efforts. [Accessed 15 December 2022]

Pg 119, *2004 Tsumani* - Wikipedia. 2022. 2004 Indian Ocean earthquake and tsunami. [ONLINE] Available at: https://en.wikipedia.org/wiki/2004_Indian_Ocean_earthquake_and_tsunami. [Accessed 15 December 2022]

Pg 184,*Dunkirk* - English Heritage. 2022. OPERATION DYNAMO: THINGS YOU NEED TO KNOW ABOUT THE DUNKIRK EVACUATION. [ONLINE] Available at: https://www.english-heritage.org.uk/visit/places/dover-castle/history-and-stories/operation-dynamo-things-you-need-to-know/. [Accessed 15 December 2022].
Wikipedia. 2022. Dunkirk evacuation. [ONLINE] Available at: https://en.wikipedia.org/wiki/Dunkirk_evacuation. [Accessed 15 December 2022]

ABOUT THE AUTHOR

Sarah Holloway is a communicator who carries a wealth of experience of sharing God's heart across stage and television through media and the arts. Newly saved, she was thrust into the limelight aged 20 to be a voice to the nations. During her early ministry, she witnessed a revivalist move of the Holy Spirit that brought thousands to God and transformed lives. Sarah is a multi-award-winning director of documentary film and has worked across an expansive range of specialisms as a film-maker, dancer, choreographer, director of theatre, teacher, coach, author, public speaker, and last (but not least!) a wife and mother.

If you have a speaking opportunity, are interested in a coaching programme, or would like to know more please email sarah@provisioncreatives.com

❝❝I have experienced personally the power of the prophetic gift God has given Sarah. A few years ago she reluctantly but faithfully shared with me an incredibly painful vision about my family circumstances with a vivid accuracy she could not possibly have known or foreseen without the direction of the Holy Spirit. Please listen closely to what she has to say in this precious book for our times.❞

Dr Roger Greene.

PROVISION CREATIVES

ProVision Creatives helps to equip and empower Christian creatives to step into their purpose, for such a time as this.

Are you a Christian Creative who knows you're called to be part of God's creative army?

Sarah founded ProVision Creatives to help you take the next step in fulfilling the creative call of God on your life. If you are called to use your God-given gifts for Kingdom purposes, then you'll discover a programme tailored just for you!

What creatives say:

"Outstanding, amazing"

"inspiring and thought provoking"

"Brill loving it ! Thanks x"

"Mind opening"

"Encouraging & Inspiring"

"Blissful Indulgence"

"Excellent"

Testimonials

"I wasn't sure what to expect from the course as I have been on so many business courses before, including Christian ones. None of them have been what I hoped they'd be, but Sarah's course has been better! Sarah's encouragement and wisdom have been so valuable to me. So excited by what God's doing amongst us creatives! Thank you for listening to God and creating this course :)"
SB (artist)

"It has been a joy so far to listen to Godly teaching especially for creatives, such a treat for us and to meet other Christian creatives with the same heart."
MH (artist)

"Had a big lump in my throat as I listened to Sarah. You have been an inspiration Sarah, more than words can say"
Anonymous (actor)

"Sarah has been a tremendous support to me. She has shown me God's Word through my challenging patches and guided me in his way. She is truthful, loving, and kind, and I highly recommend her coaching programme. Sarah encouraged me with God's word when I was thinking negatively and falsely, which helped me to get back on the right path. My connection with God has improved with Sarah's support."
AM (artist)

"Today's session was awesome, really fruitful, and encouraging. Till a few days ago I was in confusion, but after meeting with you and praying, I can't explain my joy because God has given me a clear vision."
SM (creative entrepreneur)

"Working with Sarah has been a blessing, as I was lacking a mentor in my life for a long time, and now I finally have one."
BM (filmmaker)

"When I joined the Transformational Experience for Christian Creatives I was at the end of my tether. I was procrastinating to such a degree that any creativity had gone out of the window. I was disheartened and on the verge of giving up. I have become much more settled and secure in who I am in God. Much of the frenetic and chaotic nature of my life has gone, to be replaced with a much stronger sense of who I am and how much I matter to God. Sarah is a great encourager, sensitive to the Holy Spirit and very prophetic."
KD (creative)

"Sarah was exactly who I needed as a person to confide to with matters regarding creativity and faith."
DK (writer & filmmaker)

FOR MORE INFORMATION:

Visit: **www.provisioncreatives.com**

Or Email: **sarah@provisioncreatives.com**

FURTHER READING

This book is also available in eBook and Audio Book

If you're a Christian Creative then look out for my new book (2023) written just for you... go to my ProVision Creatives website and stay connected!

It will be packed full of tips and information, especially for creatives who want to see their God-given talents and gifts used for Kingdom purpose. If you want to communicate God's heart through your creative art, then let's connect.

I hope you've enjoyed reading this book and working with the Holy Spirit to discern your part in this awesome journey of life.

All for His Glory!